BERNARD SHAW'S LETTERS
TO GRANVILLE BARKER

BERNARD SHAW'S
LETTERS TO
GRANVILLE BARKER

edited by C. B. PURDOM

with commentary and notes

THEATRE ARTS BOOKS
NEW YORK

Library of Congress Catalog Card Number: 56-9608

Published by
THEATRE ARTS BOOKS, 224 West Fourth St., New York 14

Printed in the United States of America by
The Haddon Craftsmen, Scranton, Pa.

Contents

Contents

Prefatory Note

The beginning of the art of letters is letter writing and some of the best writing of many authors is contained in their letters. That is true of Bernard Shaw who was an incessant letter writer. His first published writing was a letter to the press, and he never ceased to write to *The Times* to the end of his life. His letters are good because he took care over them, not because he thought of their publication: he had something to communicate, and he thought of his correspondent.

The letters in this book are an admirable example of his private correspondence, and are all that remain of what he wrote to Harley Granville Barker. Written at the height of his creativity as a dramatist their value lies in the presentation of the mind of a master dramatist concerned with his playwriting, and the interpretation and staging of his plays. Although all playwrights are concerned with such practical matters as Shaw deals with here, no dramatist of the first rank has left a record of practical stage work such as this. The letters start at the beginning of the century soon after meeting the man in whom Shaw had the greatest confidence as the hope of the new drama, and with whom he worked for many years. They cover the period of their active working together, continue fitfully after the break in their association, and end with the death of Charlotte Shaw.

The largest number of letters was written during the Court Theatre season when Shaw was instructing, encouraging and criticizing his friend and co-worker, the most fruitful period of both their lives. Barker's letters to Shaw have disappeared, and I am satisfied that with the exception of a few late ones they were destroyed. It is, however, possible to get an idea of the young Barker from Shaw's letters as the latter saw him, or as he allowed Barker to think he saw him.

The letters are mostly in Shaw's hand, though a few were type-written. There are some postcards, a favourite means of communication with Shaw. Those from abroad were almost invariably written on a series of picture postcards, numbered and separately stamped and posted. Despite their intimacy Shaw addressed Barker as "Barker" or "G.B.," never by his Christian name, and signed with his initials or full signature; at times he did not inscribe his letters to him.

Included in the book are some letters addressed to Barker's partner, J. E. Vedrenne, and others.

The letters are printed exactly as written, without omissions.

In the connecting narrative I have aimed at conciseness, making only such explanations as appeared necessary.

I have to acknowledge with thanks the permission of the Public Trustee and the Society of Authors for the publication of these letters.

Granville Barker's name is spelled throughout this book without a hyphen, as "Granville" was a Christian name and did not form part of his surname, though after his second marriage in 1918 he signed his name with a hyphen.

C. B. PURDOM

1

The Stage Society

The letters from Bernard Shaw to Harley Granville Barker contained in these pages start at the opening of the twentieth century and continue until Mrs. Shaw's death in 1943. They were written to the man who was most closely associated with him in his work as playwright, and whose practical knowledge of the stage was put to use and developed by him, and they form a record of a collaboration unique in the theatre of this century. The letters are mostly occupied with the practical day-to-day problems of the theatre and their solution, but they go beyond their immediate purpose and have bearing upon the work of the playwright as a whole.

When the letters start, Shaw was forty-eight years old and Barker twenty-two. Shaw was already an established dramatist having published three substantial volumes of plays containing ten works in all, of which five had been publicly performed and one censored. Two years earlier he had given up work as dramatic critic for the more serious task of dramatic craftsmanship, knowing that the two activities do not go together. Barker in 1900 was a young actor with ten years' experience of the stage, and was already an incipient dramatist. The leading dramatists on the London stage were still Arthur Wing Pinero and Henry Arthur Jones, while the domestic problem play, musical comedy, and spectacular Shakespeare productions were the popular theatrical fare. The star of Ibsen had arisen, but it was regarded as no more than a shooting star.

However, a ferment of new life was at work, the signs of which were the formation in London of a number of theatrical societies, a brief account of which must be given to introduce this cor-

respondence. The first was the Independent Theatre run by the Dutch-born dramatic critic, J. T. Grein, who had organized the production of a number of English plays in Amsterdam in 1890, and used gifts of money made to him arising from that effort to form a society in London, where he lived. Among the society's first members were George Meredith, Thomas Hardy, A. W. Pinero, H. A. Jones and Gilbert Murray; its total membership never exceeded 175. Its first production was Ibsen's Ghosts, on 9 March 1891, and its sixth, Shaw's Widowers' Houses, on 9 December 1892. "The disparagers ask what it is independent of," wrote Bernard Shaw, when the society had been going for nearly four years. "It is, of course," he added, "independent of commercial success." Altogether the Independent Theatre was responsible for 22 productions before it came to an end in 1897.

Then followed William Archer's New Century Theatre, in the spring of 1897, to further the cause of dramatic art, and to pave the way for a National Theatre in the new century, with a committee consisting of Elizabeth Robins, William Archer and H. W. Massingham, Alfred Sutro being honorary secretary, and the publisher, Gerald Duckworth, treasurer. The society grew out of a fund provided for the production of Ibsen's Little Eyolf at the Avenue Theatre the previous 23 November. Its first play was John Gabriel Borkman at the Strand Theatre on 3 May 1897, followed by Stevenson and Henley's Admiral Guinea at the Avenue Theatre on 28 November. After that the society proposed to do Ibsen's Peer Gynt, but never did so, and considered, but turned down, Henry James's one-act piece Mrs. Gracedew (afterwards made into a three-act play called The High Bid), also Edward Martyn's The Heather Field, making George Moore very cross over the rejection of the latter play. Then it did H. V. Esmond's four-act play, Grierson's Way, at the Haymarket Theatre on 7 February 1899, and afterwards became dormant.

At last came the Stage Society to perform "plays such as would be included in the repertory of any of the chief repertory theatres of the continent, but which under the prevailing conditions of the English stage had no opportunity of production in England." These words had reference to the censorship, for Ibsen's Ghosts had been censored, so had Shaw's Mrs. Warren's

2

Profession, *the latter play having also been refused by Grein's society. The Stage Society was the outcome of a circular letter sent on 8 July 1899 to about 150 persons known to be interested in dramatic art, inviting them to a meeting "to consider forming a small society for the production of plays." The letter was signed by Frederick Whelen, a Fabian, who was on the staff of the Bank of England, Charles Charrington and Janet Achurch, who had a company touring with plays by Ibsen and Shaw, Grant Richards, who was Bernard Shaw's first publisher and was related to Whelen, Walter Crane, the socialist artist, and William Sharp, the poet. At the meeting held on 19 July at Whelen's house, 17 Red Lion Square, forty to fifty people attended, and it was agreed to form a society to meet once a month and to give at least six performances throughout the year in large studios on Sunday evenings. The plays were to be without scenery in draped backgrounds, and to include "high comedy" as well as more serious works, English as well as continental. A managing committee was elected with Frederick Whelen, chairman, Ernest E. S. Williams, honorary-secretary, and Charles Charrington, Laurence Irving, William Sharp and James Welch. A reading and advisory committee was also elected, which included Mrs. Bernard Shaw. The brief rules stated that the subscription was two guineas a year, the number of members to be a minimum of two hundred and a maximum of three hundred, that tickets to the performances should not be transferable, but that each member should have the privilege of inviting one guest to each performance without further payment. Even dramatic critics were required to pay, and the "meetings" were not to be called performances. There was to be no publicity. Sunday evenings were chosen for the "meetings," so that professional actors could assist. At first it was intended that the members, who included some professional actors, should act the plays, but amateurs were not in fact ever cast for parts. No salary was offered, but all performers, whatever their parts, received the same nominal sum for expenses, which was one guinea.*

So good was the response to the appeal for membership that no studio was large enough for "meetings" and unsuccessful attempts were made to find a picture gallery or other large hall, even a

3

circus, or skating rink, all to no purpose. A theatre was not considered practicable for a Sunday performance, but in desperation the society approached the lessee of the Royalty Theatre, Dean Street, Soho, who gave permission for the first "meeting," which was a performance of Shaw's You Never Can Tell. Two years earlier the play had been turned down by Cyril Maude, after a fortnight's rehearsal at the Haymarket Theatre, because neither he nor the other actors could make anything of it. Produced for the society by the popular comedian James Welch, who also played the Waiter, and performed on Sunday 26 November, the play was an overwhelming success, and at once put the society on its feet. Though by no means a play to offend the censor, Shaw's assault upon old-fashioned and even new-fashioned ideas was much to the taste of the society's Fabian public. Indeed, its author both then and later seemed rather overcome by the unqualified approval it received; writing a few days after the performance to Ellen Terry he said, "We shall hear no more about its being a bad stage play," and added, "I was ashamed of its tricks and laughs and popularities."

Until that November night, not for hundreds of years had a play been performed in a London theatre on a Sunday, even privately, so two inspectors of police called at the Royalty Theatre before the performance to challenge its legality; but Whelen, the chairman, kept them busy disputing the matter until the play got well started. In fact, the performance was entirely legal, and the venture set going other Sunday evening play societies, and initiated what has become a regular practice of private performances on Sundays (and weekdays) for members only, not so much to do censored plays as partly to provide Sunday entertainment, and partly to perform plays in buildings that do not come up to the requirements of the licensing authorities.

At the third "meeting" of the society at the Vaudeville Theatre on 25 February 1900, Granville Barker made his first Stage Society appearance as an actor in the part of Erik Bratsberg in Ibsen's The League of Youth, and at the Globe Theatre, on 29 April, he was the producer of a programme of three short plays, Maeterlinck's Interior and The Death of Tintagiles, and Fiona MacLeod's The House of Usna. He played Robert in Ger-

4

hart Hauptmann's The Coming of Peace, *produced by Janet Achurch at the Vaudeville Theatre on 10 June, and, on 1 July, at the Strand Theatre, Eugene Marjoribanks (as the character was then called) in Bernard Shaw's* Candida, *produced by Janet Achurch, with herself as Candida, and Charles Charrington as Morell.*

Bernard Shaw had first seen Barker in the society's performance of Hauptmann's play. "I was at my wits end for an actor who could do justice to the part of Marchbanks," he said, "and instantly saw the very fellow for my poet." As Eugene, Barker's qualities as an actor were expressed to the fullest extent; his buoyant, self-conscious youthfulness matched the part, while the lyrical quality in his light voice, as well as complete absorption in the character, gave his playing elevation. Born in London on 25 November 1877, Barker had been on the stage since he was thirteen. He had toured with Ben Greet in Shakespeare from 1895 onwards, played for William Poel, and had been in Mrs. Patrick Campbell's company. The Stage Society brought the two men together, and the cornerstone was laid for Barker's subsequent career.

A proposal by the Charringtons that they should repeat the production in matinees at the Comedy Theatre was refused by Shaw, because he did not consider their performances good enough.

This play completed the society's first season. At the first annual meeting on 26 July 1900 it had been agreed to increase the maximum membership to five hundred, to give two performances of each play, the second being a week-day matinee at which the press was to be admitted, and to allocate seats by ballot conducted by scrutineers. Hitherto seats had been occupied by members as they arrived.

There follows the first letter from Shaw that Barker had preserved.

Blackdown Cottage, Haslemere.
22 Aug 1900.

Dear Barker,

I am surprised by your letter, as I have only had the photograph for about a fortnight, and I never answer a letter sooner

5

than two years. I now however make a special exception in your favor and sign the picture forthwith. My wife promises to tie it up and send it, so there is a reasonable probability of your receiving it tomorrow.

The next performance of Candida will probably take place at about the date of the final partition of China by the Powers.

Yours ever,

G. Bernard Shaw.

P.S. Why the deuce doesn't Evans do a portrait of *you* and present a copy to *me*?

This letter is characteristic of Shaw's exaggerated way of expressing himself. The Frederick J. Evans referred to was a bookseller friend of Shaw's and an amateur photographer, who specialized in photographing churches. "He is an odd little man, a wild enthusiast about music and acting," as Shaw told Ellen Terry, when he suggested she should allow him to take her. Evans photographed many of Shaw's friends.

When Ellen Terry, notwithstanding Shaw's blandishments, had finally refused to play Lady Cecily in Captain Brassbound's Conversion *it was to be performed by the society on December 16, with Janet Achurch in the part. Barker was to play the American naval officer, and was having difficulties with the part. He got this letter from Shaw:*

10, Adelphi Terrace, W. C.
6 December 1900.

Dear G.B.

Unless you can make the acquaintance of a real American and live with him night and day for the next week, that part will ruin you. It's not a question of acting: its a question of intonation. Where are we to get a captain if you give it up Heaven only knows; but I had rather have the play postponed than let you, unwarned, miss fire after your previous bulleyes. Its most extraordinarily wrong—reminds me of a performance of the Soldiers' Chorus from Faust by a Siamese native orchestra under the title of The Celestial Glory. You have the intonation of an English gentleman, and rather smart and snappy at that; and

6

the lines wont go to it: they are pure Chicagoan, not Piccadilly. For Redbrook it would be perfection; and you are much more likely to get bread and butter engagements in the Redbrook tone than in the captain's tone, which any old actor who is a good mimic and has heard enough of Chicagoan could hit off. There is no use my demonstrating what I want; for I am not a particularly good mimic; and an imitation of an imitation is a poor business. Couldnt you join an American club for a week? It's really serious; for that last act as it goes now is ruinous.

Excuse these candors; but Charrington would sacrifice you like a paschal lamb to get his cast complete. Or else he wants to create an emergency and play the captain himself—unconsciously, you understand, for consciously he is the soul of honour.

Why dont you play Drinkwater?—if you scorn Redbrook.

Yr ever

G. Bernard Shaw.

The few rehearsals were not at all satisfactory to the dramatist as can be seen from a further letter. Redbrook, played by Roland Bottomley, was a part Shaw had first thought of for Barker. Courtenay Thorpe was a member of Charrington's company and had played Eugene in Candida *on tour, as well as many Ibsen parts; "an actor of the highest class in modern drama" was Shaw's judgment.*

10, Adelphi Terrace, W.C.
7th December 1900.

Dear G.B.

9.10 be blowed! I was not down to my own porridge until 9.20, and was late for the rehearsal in consequence. By the kindness of Providence several excellent actors walked into the theatre shortly afterwards and took Drinkwater, Sidi and the Sheikh off our hands, Thorpe playing Sir Howard.

I believe you must play that fatheaded captain after all; but by the Lord it will be a disgraceful outrage on nature. You are about as fit to play him as I am to write Besant's novels. Your divine gifts of youth, delicacy and distinction will be murdered; and so will the part. However, I cant write in another Eugene for you; and you will have to do the captain *with your head,* unless Bottomley will take Marzo and leave you—but that wont do; for where are we to get our captain, unless the Cadi doubles him. (The Cadi, by the way, turns out to be the part in the piece). No: youve got to play the captain, spite of dead cats, bottles, turnips, putrid eggs, and authors. Kismet!

G. Bernard Shaw.

Ellen Terry came to the performance. ". . . oh, shan't we enjoy it all. I'm going off my head," she wrote to the author. They met there for the first time. Shaw's candid criticism of Barker's performance is contained in the following letter. In fact, Barker had not wanted to play the part or any part in the play.

Piccard's Cottage, St. Catherine's
Guildford.
2nd Jan. 1901.

Dear Granville Barker,

The only thing I regret about the Sunday performance (I wasnt at the Thursday one) is that I was so close to the Stage that your makeup, which so fascinated Archer, was lost on me. My only misgiving with regard to you is as to whether the Stage, in its present miserable condition, is good enough for you: you are sure to take to authorship or something of the kind. Meanwhile, however, you give me the *quality* of work I want; and I hope to get some more of it out of you before you get tired of it.

Have you read Rostand's L'Aiglon? Now that is a part you ought to play before you get middleaged. I wonder would Rostand allow us to perform it in consideration of our really standing by his play instead of making it a stalking horse for a battered old showwoman.

Yours ever
G. Bernard Shaw.

The Philanderer, written as long ago as 1893, was being considered by the society, but the difficulty was an actress for the part of Julia. It is not an easy play to cast, but there were other

8

difficulties, and the play was never liked by Shaw's friends. The projected performance fell through and the play was not done until six years later at the Court Theatre. The letter to Barker shows Shaw consulting his friend and valuing his opinion.

10, Adelphi Terrace, W.C.
29th October 1901.

I agree about Constance Collier for Julia: we must have somebody who is overpowering. Failing her, what do you think of Mrs. Cecil Raleigh? Edward Rose suggests her as a possible Mrs. Warren; but I think Julia is more in her line. Miss Fraser is exactly right for Grace; and Miss McIntosh is not opulent enough —not pigmented deeply enough—for Julia, though if we have to fall back on cleverness we cannot do better. My private opinion, however, is that the part will be taken at short notice three days before the performance by Miss Janet Achurch.

I write this on the assumption that you have a committee this afternoon.

G.B.S.

Neither Shaw nor Barker took any part in the society except for committee work during 1901, though both of them had joined the managing committee at the second annual meeting. At the meeting, too, in addition to the five hundred ordinary members, one hundred associate members were allowed, the subscriptions for ordinary members being two guineas for one ticket for each production, and three guineas for two tickets, the tickets being for any part of the house other than the gallery as were to be determined by ballot. Associate members were to pay one guinea for the gallery seats for each production. The tickets were to be transferable.

The committee work, however, was very serious, for Mrs. Warren's Profession had been announced for 8 and 9 December, the Strand Theater having been promised for those dates by Frank Curzon, the manager. When he learned that the play was banned Curzon withdrew his permission. Then twelve other theatres were refused in succession, also the Cecil, Savoy and De Keyser's hotels and two picture galleries, but at last the Royal

Society of British Artists agreed to lend its gallery in Suffolk
Street, but withdrew when it realized that one of the performances
was to be on a Sunday. So three week-day performances were
arranged, the first to be on Monday 9 December, and the pro-
grammes were printed and the tickets sent out. Then Madge
McIntosh, who was to play Vivie, found she could not attend
and the performances had to be cancelled.

Finally the first performance was arranged for Sunday 5 Janu-
ary 1902 at the New Lyric Club, Coventry Street. Barker was to
play the part of Frank; Miss Fanny Brough, Mrs. Warren. Shaw
writes about Barker's work at rehearsals.

10, Adelphi Terrace, W.C,
31/12/01.

Dear G.B.

You are losing sight in the last act of the new attitude of
Vivie, hard as nails, and fiercely intolerant of any approach to
poetry. Being of a poetic turn yourself, you have a constant
tendency to modulate into E flat minor (which is short for
Eugene flat minor) which is steadily lowering the tone of Frank,
until he seems fairly likely to end as Hamlet. Instead of being
incorrigibly good-for-nothing, you are incorrigibly the other
thing. I have serious thoughts of having you to dinner on
Sunday and making you very drunk; only I fear that you would
become pious in your cups instead of gay. Instead of getting
boundless amusement out of everything disastrous, you become
the man of sorrows at every exhibition of human fraility, and
seem to be bitterly reproaching me all through for the flippancy
of my dialogue. Two rehearsals more, and you will draw tears
even in the third act.

There is one passage which is particularly dreadful because it
has absolutely no sense unless its mood is perfectly conveyed.
"What do Y O U say, govnor, eh?" You express neither curiosity
nor amusement here; and far from singing "good Old Crofts"
like a lark in the heavens, you convey the impression that you
know the man well and habitually talk of him and to him in
that way.

In short, you need not be afraid of overdoing the part: the

real danger is underdoing it. You have a frightful air of a youth in love—with Ann Leete probably.

It is a question of feeding, perhaps: you must come to lunch oftener.

When I was unable today to conceal the shock with which I saw you suddenly hit on the idea of playing that scene with Vivie exactly like the scene with Prossy in Candida, you sank into despair like a man whose loftiest inspiration has been quenched and whose noblest motives brutally misunderstood.

IT was really the fault of your cold, not mine. You nearly made Miss Brough cry.

It only wants lifting the least bit in the world. You should soar not gravitate. If you let the part weigh on your mind much more, you will find yourself breaking into the Seven Ages of Man on the night.

You got my card about the Hotel Cecil, I presume.

We begin tomorrow with the fourth act—Vivie and Frank.

G.B.S.

The performance took place before an excited audience; the club provided a stage in name only, which was a handicap upon the players. Shaw produced the play himself, and after a performance that delighted him, he was able, as he said afterwards, "to step on the stage and apply the strong words genius to the representation with the certainty of electing an instant and overwhelming assent from the audience." After the performance an edition of the play was published with twelve photographs by Frederick J. Evans and a long preface. Shaw gave a copy to "Frank the First."

A little more than three weeks later, on 26 January, Barker's own play The Marrying of Ann Leete *(referred to in the above letter) was performed at the Royalty Theatre, the author producing. No letter survives from Shaw on this production, but other letters show that Shaw thought highly of the play.*

There was nothing more for the society from either Shaw or Barker until Barker played the principal part in Somerset Maugham's first play A Man of Honour *on 22 February 1903, afterwards appearing in a version of a play by Herman Heijermans on 26 April called* The Good Hope, *and on 7 June he produced three short plays.*

Shaw had been taken off on holiday abroad by that indefatigable traveller his wife. From the next letter it is possible to guess that Barker had written to him about Gordon Craig's production of The Vikings, *which opened at the Imperial Theatre on 15 April 1903.* The Admirable Bashville *was to be done by the Stage Society on 7 June, and Shaw writes to his friend who was to be responsible for the production.*

Grand Albergo Belle Arti, Orvieto.
23rd April 1903.

Dear Granville Barker,
Many thanks for your graphic letter. After all, one knew that that must be the result; but still one asks every time, none the less, whether the miraculous hasnt happened at last.

I do not mind Bashville being produced as a clear extra to end up the season; but it is not a burlesque. It should be announced simply as Bernard Shaw's celebrated drama in blank verse entitled *The Admirable Bashville or Constancy Rewarded,* being the only authorized dramatic version of the authors famous novel entitled "Cashel Bryon's Profession." "If you have tears, prepare to shed them now." Shakespear.

Here follows the cast

The audience is neither requested nor expected to remain seated until the fall of the curtain.

Children in arms will find this play peculiarly suited to their taste and capacity.

Copies of the play, including the novel and several prefaces, as published by Mr. Grant Richards, cannot be obtained at the box office.

The play is not produced under the personal direction of the author, who disclaims all responsibility for the performance, and, if called, will not risk an appearance before the curtain.

12

The dresses are from the private wardrobes of the performers, or have been lent by their personal friends.

The scenery is not by Mr. Gordon Craig.

As the incidental music has not yet been composed, it has been thought well to omit it.

Owing to the length of the speeches and the lateness of the hour, encores cannot be accepted.

A collection will not be taken after the glove fight in the second act.

The audience is begged to disperse quietly at the conclusion of the piece.

And any other nonsense that may occur to anybody.

G.B.S.

P.S. We are at our furthest point (Orvieto) now. We shall stay a day or two, then come north to Siena for another day or two, and then home.

Although the author was to have nothing to do with The Admirable Bashville, *he none the less paid much attention to it.*

Maybury Knoll, Woking.
26th May 1903.

Dear Barker,

I have now looked through Bashville and find him most expensive. We shall want a crowd, including policeman and chiefs, also the following props.

A rapidly portable dais and throne for Catewayo.

Various birdwhistles, including a cuckoo.

Goblet and wine vase of gilt pasteboard on massive salver.

A large key (Lydia's door key to put down Cashel's back)

A knockout sceptre for Catewayo, not too unwieldy for a broadsword combat with Lucian's umbrella.

Softnosed spears for the chiefs.

Four enormous boxing gloves stuffed with feathers (eider down preferred).

A property posthorn.

A mossgrown tree trunk for Lydia to sit on, not too low, and really round, so that she can get her heels well under herself

13

when Cashel lifts her with one finger under her chin.

An umbrella for Lucian to fight with, as he cannot reasonably be asked to sacrifice his own.

And several trees, in tubs or otherwise.

Then as to costumes.

A white beaver hat for Mellish

A gorgeous livery with tags, plush smalls, calves, and a heavily powdered wig for Bashville. The wig is important, as when he says O Bathos! in his great soliloquy he must strike his head and send up a cloud of powder from it.

A blue handkerchief with white spots, large enough to tie round Cashel's waist, passing under the front flap of his breeches.

A crimson or yellow handkerchief for Paradise.

One break must be made at the end of the Agricultural Hall scene. If Henrietta Watson happens to have a blue dress with white spots on it she might pay Cashel a touching compliment by changing to it hastily during the break, which need not be a long one.

I am calculating on the traverses; so that unless the stage is like this I shall be stumped.

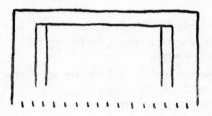

I am terrified by the length of the thing, considering the need for slow delivery and the constant making of elocutionary points. If we can coach the company up to the mark they will be able to amaze the public in Shakespeare for ever after: its splendid practice.

G.B.S.

We come up to town tomorrow. Come to lunch and report progress.

14

No producer's name was put on the programme, but the performance was a huge success. The policeman in the play, acted by Aubrey Smith, was made up to look like the author.

In 1903, however, a much more important event took place. Shaw completed and published Man and Superman, *and Barker wanted it for the society, for he saw himself as Tanner. Shaw's reply was:*

Springburn, Strachur, Argyllshire.

20/8/03.

I will autograph the copy when I return. I purposely put you on Constable's journalists list, as they might use it for other books about the theatre.

M. & S. would do excellently for the S.S. with you as Octavius, Tree as Tanner, Mrs. Charles Calvert as Mrs. Whitefield, Paul Arthur as Hector, Beveridge as Malone, Aubrey Smith as Mendoza, Welch as the Anarchist, Fennessey as Ramsden (failing Cyril Maude), Straker by Dan Leno, Violet by Mabel Terry Lewis, and Margaret Halston as Ann.

G.B.S.

This was Shaw's idea of the ideal cast, Barker being in a secondary part. The Stage Society did not do the play until it was prepared for the Court Theatre two years later, but the society was allowed the first performance.

Barker did no more playing or producing for the society until 26 June 1904 when he produced W. B. Yeats's Where There Is Nothing, *its twenty-seventh production, at the Court Theatre. At that theatre the society was afterwards allowed the credit of the first performance of* Man and Superman *on 21 May 1905, in which Barker played Tanner, an event that will be described in later letters. Except for Barker's own censored play,* Waste, *given in the programme of the society on 24 November 1907 this was the end of his active connection with the Stage Society. There was no further play from Bernard Shaw except the above-mentioned* Man and Superman. *He and his wife had become in 1904 the society's only two life members, paying twenty guineas each for the privilege. When* The Shewing-up of Blanco

15

Posnet *was censored, the Irish Players, who had produced the play publicly in Dublin, brought it to the Aldwych Theatre on 5 December 1909 on the invitation of the society. Also, to complete the story of Shaw's active participation as dramatist in the work of the society, two short pieces were afterwards given their first London production on its stage,* Augustus Does His Bit *at the Court Theatre on 21 January 1917, and* O'Flaherty, V.C. *at the Lyric Theatre on 19 December 1920.*

Although the society continued its work, the impetus of its remarkable early seasons was diminishing. Its pioneering work was in fact completed when the Vedrenne-Barker management was formed in 1904. What the society had set out to justify, the play of literary quality dealing with real life in place of the stereotyped stage versions of life, had been achieved. Not yet were the drama and stage reformed, but how reform could be achieved had been demonstrated by the creation of new dramatists and a new audience. The society expired in 1939. The London theatre today is the heir to its work.

The Vedrenne-Barker Management

Barker was keeping on at Shaw about bringing Candida *before the London public, with the dramatist keeping on the brake. Shaw was all for the idea, but discouraged the actor until the right company and favorable conditions were available.*

Kate Rorke, mentioned in the following letter, was a highly experienced actress, who had for years been in Charles Wyndham's company, and afterwards was leading lady for John Hare; she did in fact play Candida when the matinees came off during the following April. "Tith" was George S. Titheredge, who had played for the Stage Society. Madge McIntosh, a young actress, was the first Vivie in Mrs. Warren's Profession *in 1902.*

Strachur, Argyllshire.
2nd Sept. 1903.

Dear Barker,

Kate Rorke's equivalent in the new generation would certainly hit off Candida very well; but whether Kate herself would take kindly to it is another matter. I have never found a single case in which the heros and heroines of the eighties were of any use to us. The comedic geniuses, yes: the leading ladies and gentlemen, no. The more winningly natural they were in their own line, the more appallingly artificial and subconsciously recalcitrant they are in ours. Candida is not half such a chance for Kate as Lady Cicely was for Ellen Terry; and yet you see that Ellen dared even Ibsen (the Bedford Park Ibsen) sooner, and, if that had not been forced on her by Ted, would have produced a play by Clo Graves.

As to Eugene, he cant be acted; it is a question of being the creature or at least having him in you; so that the casting of Eugene is either an insuperable difficulty or, as in your case, no difficulty at all as long as you keep your figure. But Eugene cannot save the play, though he can damn it unless the others can create the necessary environment. Burgess must be thoroughly and richly amusing (Lionel Brough at least) and Prossy must be thoroughly snappy and lively, as well as the Morells being very sympathetic. Tith could manage Morell (though I shouldnt have supposed it if I hadnt seen him in Beyond Human Power) but not with anything to spare.

Why dont you propose the play to Mrs. Pat? She once asked for it; but at that time my promise to let Janet have the first bite in London was unfulfilled; and I had to excuse myself. At the same time, Mrs. Pat would not be a bit Candida; but she would help you with her prestige; and her cleverness would carry her very far in it. Mrs. Kendal and Kendal would be ideal if only they were of our generation; but, as in Kate's case, they would rebel against it in their hearts; and Mrs. Kendal would make points to help the lame dog over the stile.

I don't want to sit on the play in the very least: it is ancient history for me now. But I don't think your position would be improved unless it were an unequivocal success, because, as I have already said, not only can Eugene not save the play himself, but the part would become harsh, ridiculous, and even violently unpopular if it were wrongly supported. It is useless to be impatient, especially with your present prosperous engagement.

What did you make of Trebitsch?

I have read—or rather re-read—Edward II. Had I done so two months ago I should have advised you strongly not to wipe out Richard II by playing it. There is nothing in it—no possibility of success; and the infernal tradition that Marlowe was a great dramatic poet instead of a XVI century Henley throws all the blame for his wretched half-achievement on the actor. Marlowe had words and a turn for their music, but nothing to say—a barren amateur with a great air.

G.B.S.

Whoever she may be; but Madge McIntosh is much more in our line. Have you thought of her?

Shaw's critical appreciation of leading London West End actors and actresses is especially to be noted; what he says in the above letter was no casual remark but expressed a view he always held. He found only a few to be of use in his plays, able to give the kind of full-blooded acting he called for. This is further shown by his suggesting Mrs. Patrick Campbell for Candida, for, as he says, she would not have been Candida, but would have displayed the energy he valued. Barker had been in Mrs. Pat's company on tour. Ellen Terry had "dared even Ibsen" when The Vikings *was produced by her son at her Imperial Theatre the previous April. Clotilde Innez Mary Graves was an Irish-born-writer of light verse and popular comedies, and under the name of Richard Dehan, a best-selling novelist. The Austrian, Siegfried Trebitsch, was the translator of Shaw's plays into German. Marlowe's* Edward II *had been produced the previous month at Oxford by William Poel with Barker in the name part. Shaw disliked all Elizabethans except Shakespeare, a dislike Barker adopted from him.*

The casting problems were being considered, Shaw making as many difficulties as possible. "V" in the following letter was Sidney Valentine, considered to be an excellent actor, but not the man for Morell, or, as Shaw thought, for his plays at all.

Strachur, 24/9/03.
V. is just the man Kate would think right for Morell. He is "strong" in a highly actorian's way. If found in Victoria Park he would be shot as a strange animal. Asche has the sort of human humor about him, the big baby sort of power, that is wanted for Morell, who, by the way, must not be a churchy parson. V. would make the whole part a funeral service. Forbes R. would be laic in comparison. I should say in fairness that I have not seen V. since Capt. Brassb. and then not acting but at a rehearsal at which Charrington tried to tempt him with the judge's part. I blew the gaff as to its glories, and V. fled.

I had seen him act: it was not bad of its kind; but its kind was exactly indicated by his romantic name.

G.B.S.

At last the chance came. J. H. Leigh, a well-off amateur actor, who had backed Martin Harvey in the original production of The Only Way, *became lessee of the Royal Court Theatre in Sloane Square, and put on a series of "Shakespeare Representations," starting in October 1903, for which J. E. Vedrenne was engaged as manager, and in April the following year Granville Barker was engaged to produce* The Two Gentlemen of Verona, *in which he also played Speed. He made it part of the arrangement that he should give six matinees of* Candida.

Shaw continued to throw cold water on Barker's hot enthusiasm, which was "hideous folly." Shaw's insistence on what he wanted in the acting of the play was characteristic.

Strathur, 27/9/03.

(On the 30th we go to the Central
Station Hotel, Glasgow, until the
5th.)

Unless every advertisement is headed TUESDAYS THURSDAYS and FRIDAYS in colossal print the scheme will fail because people will get confused about the dates, which are perfectly idiotic. Or am I to understand that there are to be no press advertisements—only circulars? £300 aint much for 12 matinees. My percentages are, on the gross, not exceeding £50 = 5%, not exceeding £100 = 7½%, exceeding £100 = 10%. This does not mean 5% on the first £50, 7½ on the next and 10 on the rest: if the gross is £51 I get 7½ on the £51, if £101 I get 10% on the £101. But before I consent to such a hideous folly as it all appears to be, I must know who the people are. We must not get mixed up with people who will run into debt and shoot the moon. Who is the Margot lady? Graham Browne is too good—too heavy—for Lexy, isn't he? I am not convinced about Volpe: Burgess is *very* important. Is Anson still alive and possible? Thats the sort of thing the part wants. Or Lionel Brough.

G.B.S.

The six matinees started on April 26, with Kate Rorke as Candida, Norman McKinnel as Morell, and Barker, of course, as Eugene. The result was satisfactory. Unknown, perhaps, to her husband, Mrs. Shaw had guaranteed the finance up to £160, which was not required. Much interest was aroused—"capital sport!" was Walkley's comment in his appreciation of the play, while William Archer said that the play proved "that Mr. Shaw possesses in a high degree the specific gifts of the dramatist. If only he could keep in check, and subdue to artistic uses, the multiplicity of his other gifts, he might be one of the leading playwrights of Europe." Among Shaw's multiplicity of other gifts was one for politics, and this production of Candida coincided with the end of his activities in local government, for he had been rejected by the electors of St. Pancras as a representative of the borough on the newly formed London County Council the year before. He had resigned from the Borough Council, on which he had served (including the earlier vestry) for six years, devoting much time to the work. There follows Shaw's receipt for his fees:

10, Adelphi Terrace, W.C.
11 June 1904.

Received from H. Granville Barker Esq. the sum of Thirtyone pounds three shillings stg being the amount of authors fees due to me for six performances of "Candida" at the Court Theatre on April 26th and 29th and May 3rd, 5th, 6th, 10th, as verbally agreed between us.

G. Bernard Shaw
11/6/04.

As the Candida matinees yielded a profit, an attempt to inaugurate a regular season of matinees seemed to be justified, so the Vedrenne-Barker management came into being. That would hardly have been possible had not J. H. Leigh been highly favourable to the project, to which he gave not only his blessing but practical support. Finance was secured as required from a number of friends in comparatively small sums.

Bernard Shaw had had an earlier experience of the Court

Theatre, for it was there that A. W. Pinero's Trelawny of the Wells
*was produced, on 20 January 1898, when Shaw was a dramatic
critic. The management did not send tickets to the* Saturday
Review *for this production, and its critic had to purchase a seat
for the fourth performance. Shaw wrote one of his best critical
articles of his entire career on this play, declaring that "it has
touched me more than anything else Mr. Pinero has written," but
he laid-about the actors in a forthright way.*

*It is worth remembering that Shaw was averse to the practice
of managers supplying free seats to editors for their critics or
anyone else. He considered that critics should pay for their seats,
and had devoted an article two years earlier to the subject, saying, "The complimentary invitation system is pure, unmitigated,
indefensible corruption and blackmail."*

*It was Shaw's idea that the Vedrenne-Barker matinees to be
started in November should open with* Captain Brassbound's
Conversion, *with Ellen Terry as Lady Cecily, but she could not
do it. Granville Barker wanted* Man and Superman, *but Shaw
would not listen. Instead, he held out the possibility of the new
play about Ireland upon which he was working.*

The Old House, Harmer Green, Welwyn.

4th August 1904.

I think the Superman would need a cast of more weight and
splendour than Rule Britannia (provisional name for the Irish
play). But the casting will be difficult enough in both cases. I
think you will have to play Larry, Nina Boucicault Nora (who
now has a tearing emotional scene), Oscar Asche Broadbent,
Jimmy Welch Keegan, J. L. Shine the priest, Dick Purdon the
stage Irishman, Beveridge Cornelius Doyle, and a specially engaged Irishman to double Barney Doran, Patsy and Haffigan, unless Hendrie and Kinghorne can do brogues.

G.B.S.

*In August Shaw's wife took him for a holiday to Scotland while
he was working on the Irish play, but he did not enjoy it. He
was writing away furiously but could not get on with the play
because of holiday discomforts: "Oh these holidays, these ac-*

cursed holidays!" While there he had to write a curtain-raiser for Arnold Daly, the American actor who had made his name playing Eugene in Candida *in New York. He polished off the little play in four days, calling it* How He Lied to Her Husband.

Alness. 12th August 1904.

Our expedition has been so far a ruinous failure. The place is impossible—no place to write—no place to bathe—the inn a new tumor on an old public house in a village shed—the firth a sludgy morass except at high tide. The journey wrecked me; put me out of my stride; lost me four days work for nothing. Oh these holidays, these accursed holidays! Now Charlotte must go forth and find me a possible habitation, whilst I abandon Rule Britt. to write a curtain-raiser for Daly, who writes to say that he wants to produce it at latest on the 10th. Sept.!!! There is no comfort in your list. I think, however, that I may have the play finished early in September.

G.B.S.

Six days later, Shaw in better mood had found the title for the new play, John Bull's Other Island. *He wanted Barker for the important role of Larry, but he would not do it.*

Alness.
18th August 1904.

Dear Barker,

I have polished off Daly in four days with a screaming curtain raiser entitled How He Lied to Her Husband, specialized for a theatre at which Candida has been raging, and for an actor who has played Eugene. It will do very well at the Court as a curtain raiser to The Man of Destiny, if you can induce Mrs. Pat to play the Strange Lady: otherwise I cannot very decently betray Margaret, and you will have to put up with her.

What do you think of John Bull's Other Island as a title for Rule Britannia? I can think of nothing better. I resumed work on it this morning, and am within a dozen speeches of the end. The cheapest Broadbent I can think of is George; but Asche would be burlier and better. What about Graham Browne for

23

one of the Irish parts? If Hendrie and Kinghorne can put up brogues, they would do very well. Shine and Graham Browne (G.B. as Patsy Farrell, I fancy) would complete a decent Irish quartet. Welch as Keegan (but he is New Clowning in New-castle and probably wouldn't be manageable) and you as Larry would fit in very well. Where are we to get an elderly Irish-woman for Aunt Judy?—*not* Kate Kearney. Is Mrs. Herbert Waring Irish? Nora is a miserable creature: I fear Nina would scorn her.

We move tomorrow to the Hawkhill Marine Hotel, Rose-markie, Fortrose N.B. to which address all communications until further notice.

Yr

G.Bernard Shaw.

P.S. The scenes required are 1 The Bloomsbury flat, 2 the cricket scene, 3 the round tower (which might be faked with the same back cloth), 4 a cottage garden with practicable cottage porch, 5 a cottage interior, changing to No. 2, which is the final scene. Better hire the lot.

Some extras will be wanted for the fourth act—all men, say half a dozen.

The Irish play was written with the Abbey Theatre in mind, but it got far beyond what was possible in Dublin. All the dramatist's energies were concentrated upon this new play, and though Barker was still angling after Man and Superman *with which to open his Court Theatre season Shaw had the idea of making the opening play his new piece. His ideas of a cast were good, but only one of the actors mentioned was in the original production, and in another part: J. L. Shine, who played Larry. J. D. Beveridge came into the company later, when he played Father Dempsey.*

The astute Shaw was concerned about the date of the opening. It must not be until after Parliament had met in November, and of course he was right.

Firthview, Rosemarkie,
Fortrose N.B.
20/8/04.

It has only just occurred to me that it would be very bad business to produce Rule Britt. before parliament meets again. In
fact, it mustn't be done. You will sell a lot of stalls to the
political people; and the Irish M.P.s will fill the pit. I forget
the exact date of the next session—early in November, I think.

The revision threatens to take longer than I thought. After
two days hard, I am not yet *half way through the first act*.

I am sending a card concerning the date to Vedrenne.

G.B.S.

As will be seen Shaw was keen on reviving Widowers' Houses.
The Weather Hen *was a comedy by Berte Thomas and Granville
Barker, produced at Terry's Theatre on 29 June 1899, in which
Madge McIntosh had made a good appearance, and the piece had
been much praised. Brandon Thomas was the author of, and
leading player in,* Charley's Aunt *(1892)*.

Firthview, Rosemarkie,
Fortrose N.B.
21st Aug. 1904.

If by any chance Brandon Thomas happens to be out of a
first class engagement this winter, could you tempt him to come
to the Court? He could play any part in John Bull better than
timehonored Lancaster. Madge McIntosh has asked Daly for an
engagement. If she doesn't get it (and it is surely too late now,
except perhaps for Mrs. Warren next spring) you might keep
Widowers' Houses in your mind as a possible treat to vary your
program with. She and G.B. do it extremely well. Then there
is the Old Weather Hen, which I never saw, and which she
would be glad to have another go at. She would also come in
handy for How He Lied &c, the curtain raiser for Destiny,
which ought not to have the Strange Lady played by the same
woman as the other as the monotony would be intolerable.

G.B.S.

*John Bull's Other Island, still unfinished, was to start re-
hearsals on 15 September; the play was done not on 18 October
but a fortnight later.*

Firthview, Rosemarkie, Fortrose N.B.

24th August 1904.

We shall probably stay here for some time, if not for all the
time. I finished the first draft of the play yesterday, and began
the revision and staging this morning. There is no ending at
all: only a transcendental conversation which will stagger the
very soul of Vedrenne and send the audience away howling.
Larry is now a very unsympathetic part, and is not at all an
actor's treasure, Keegan being the serious star and Broadbent
the comic one. You may have to play Keegan after all. France
might play Larry if he is destitute enough to want a job. Rule
Britannia will not do; it is too frankly a jest; and we shall have
to play off the piece as a very advanced and earnest card in the
noble game of elevating the British theatre. I am too busy to
write to Vedrenne yet: I must cram all sail on to finishing the
staging and getting the prompt copies typed. I have little hope
of reaching that haven much before the 10th. Sept.

If the first performance is to be on the 18th. Oct. we should
not begin rehearsing much later than the 15th. at latest; and it
would be better to begin on the 3rd, which will mean a re-
heasal *every day*. If the cast is otherwise engaged and wants
Wednesdays and Saturdays off &c &c, then the production must
be postponed, or else I must lose my holiday or die; for remember
that I have been working like ten galley slaves all the time down
here and I must get a lazy fortnight before I attack the rehearsals.

G.B.S.

*The play was postponed as Shaw wished. Problems of casting
loom in his mind. It is evident that Barker was not willing to
play Keegan. Shaw's ideas are practical, detailed and highly interesting. In the following letter Lillah McCarthy is mentioned
for the first time: it seems that Barker must have proposed her
for the part of Nora, for he already knew her, they having played*

together in Ben Greet's company years before, and Shaw remembered and admired her too, though he had not met her after the long past amateur performance as Lady Macbeth. Later on she did play the part, but the first Nora was Ellen O'Malley. Daniel McCarthy is referred to again in another letter. Shaw's intention of doing a play about Cromwell did not proceed further. He is trying to bring up Barker in the way he would have him go.

Firthview, Rosemarkie, Fortrose, N.B.
28th August 1904.

Dear Barker,

Attention!

There are 12 people in the cast. I do not think any of them need be expensive people. I renounce Brandon Thomas: there is nothing worth his salary.

There are 6 male dialect Irish parts. One of them, the stage Irishman, who does not reappear after the first act, might be done by, say, Neville Doone, if he can sling the dialect.

Patsy Farrell is a young, silly, flaxen polled, mossy headed Irish lad. If you could achieve the brogue, you might play him as a variation on Speed. For him I suggest Graham Browne.

The two parts in this dialect set which will be coveted, and create jealousy as to the lead in that line, are Matt. Haffigan, an old, small, peat faced, leathery man with a very deep plaintively surly voice, and Barney Doran, a coarse, red haired reckless man of barbarous humor. Haffigan has his chance in the third act (he does not reappear); and Doran has what will be professionally considered the fattest bit—the story of the pig in the first scene of Act IV. I should give Beveridge Doran as he is veteran enough to be entitled to the best bit. I confess I dont quite see Shine as Haffigan: who would suit Kinghorne better if K were an Irishman; but we shall want Shine anyhow either for that, or for Father Dempsey. He would be good as the priest; but the job is rather too small for him. Failing Beveridge, he or Wilfred Shine might play Doran. Failing Wilfred, Hendrie—always if he can cackle appropriately. Corney Doyle, an elderly, careworn, country town man of business, pre-

27

sents no difficulty and needs no big salary. I have not thought of anybody in particular for him. Query, Charrington?

Hodson stands by himself. Clarence, Trollope, Brookfield, Playfair, anybody who can do the conventional valet and break out a bit in the third act. Not, observe, a butler like Volpe; but a valet.

Keegan is a part apart. One suggestion will surprise you. I believe Shine (J. L.) could be made do it; but this is by the way for the present. The age presents no difficulty, because Keegan is not an aged or heavy man. For instance, if you had to play Newman, or even Leo XIII, you would need only the makeup. Kyrle Bellew, Harry Irving, Courtenay Thorpe (!) Forbes Robertson, could all do it with a wrinkle and a touch of powder. So you need not funk Keegan's years. I do not know whether so unsentimental a Roman as you are could possibly catch the patriotic emotion of Keegan, with his island of the saints; but if I were you I think I should try.

Now as to Broadbent and Larry. George's fitness depends on whether he is clever enough to give a new, robust, Aschelike version of his Harelite old gent in Tarpey's Windmills. There is a rather overwhelming love scene where he carries Nora off her feet by mere depth of chest, so to speak. Asche could do it; but I know nobody else; and if it must be faked, George might fake it as well as another. It is essentially a character part. Goodhart has the physique for it; so has Maurice; but—! What can Playfair do? Anything in that line? Is Calvert capable of character acting? Cyril Maude would do it enormously—some of it; but he could only do superlatively well the bits that George could do well enough. Broadbent's a difficulty. We certainly do want Asche for it very badly.

As to Larry, I see nobody better than France. But if France could do Broadbent (I have seen him only in Les Bienafiteurs, which he played Larrylike—altogether without the sanguine geniality which is the soul of Broadbent) then we might chuck you into Larry and J. L. Shine into Keegan and worry through. My own feeling is that Broadbent is not in France's line.

Finally, as to the woman. I cannot for the life of me recall G. Ffolliott, though I have seen her often enough. One concludes that Dolores Drummond could do it on her head. But I am quite disposed to give Freda Bramleigh a chance. My wild suggestion of Mrs. Waring was based on her Gina in The Wild Duck, which was very good.

Nina Boucicault must be impossible, as Hare is touring with Little Mary; and I presume Nina is with him. Lillah is a frightful temptation: my heart cries Yes By All Means; but there will be grave risk of a scandal. She is a gorgeous creature: I could almost make another Rehan of her. By the way, would her brother be of any use? Can Ellen O'Malley play an Irish part naturally? I wonder! I have no other suggestions ready.

Poulton seems not to be fittable. Blake Adam's name conveys nothing to me except association with Benjamin Franklin and Washington.

I have not thought of any better title than John Bull's Other Island. But I dont mind its being announced as Vedrenne's Folly.

I anticipated the difficulty about postponement; so I have told the Daily Mail that it *will* be postponed until parliament meets. This answers your remark about the need for more paragraphs. A.D.M. man wrote to me begging for particulars, Vedrenne having put him on to it. I sent an interview, nominally about Daly, but really about the Irish play.

Remember that the new piece How He Lied to Her Husband is immediately available to make up a program with The Man of Destiny.

I want to write a one act piece called The Death of Cromwell. Cromwell and Napoleon would make a splendid historical program. Also a triple bill

How He Lied
Cromwell *or* Napoleon
Bashville.

for Vedrenne's benefit, with V. as Catewayo.

I am writing this after dinner, which is sheer suicide. The pace is telling heavily on me: I am not sanguine as to the 10th; and I see no difficulty whatever about a postponement or ten postponements, except your Italian origin. When you go to

Italy you will find that the waiter, though a most pleasant and social fellow, will be very unlike an English waiter in one important respect. The English waiter waits for orders, carries them out, does not anticipate them; and is neither surprised nor incommoded when you change your mind. The Italian waiter forms the strongest preconception of where you are going to sit and what you are going to have; and if you attempt to upset his expectations he knifes you. Hence your attachment to your arbitrary and totally premature dates.

Keep me advised of your changes of address.

G.B.S.

Writing the stage directions, which Shaw intended for the reader, but also for himself as producer, if not for the actors, took him much longer than the dialogue, as he admits here. In fact, the change of scene in the second act was avoided.

Firthview, Rosemarkie, Fortrose.
31st August 1904.

What is there at the Court in the way of machinery? Is there any? A hydraulic bridge would be worth its weight in radium to use for the change in the second act. At all events there will be no difficulty about a cut in the stage at the upper entrance, will there?

I am quite appalled by the slowness of my progress in revising and staging the play. It positively takes longer than writing it. I have not yet finished the second act.

A letter has just come from the Daily Mail to say that the interview is in today's issue.

G.B.S.

At last the Irish play was completed and called John Bull's Other Island. *The author had found that after revision the play contained about 32,000 words of dialogue, as he says on 7 September. "Cut it all you can," he wrote to Barker before rehearsals started. The letters concerning this play are some of the best in the collection.*

30

Jubilee Cottage, Rosemarkie, Fortrose.

7th Sept. 1904.   N.B.

I am sending the play to Miss Dickens by this post. To my horror I find on a rough computation that the thing contains about 32,000 words of dialogue; and Henry Arthur Jones, if I recollect right, puts 18,000 as the correct length. I am too floored to attempt cutting as yet. On Sunday I tried to get a holiday, and got four hours rowing instead in a hideous tempest against wind and tide. This and a long series of little contretemps here have wrecked me; and I must rest or die; for if I turn over in bed without great care my heart stops for half an hour. This comes of writing plays against time.

I am instructing Miss Dickens to send a copy direct to you at York Buildings. If this address is wrong, send me a wire. She is not likely to deliver this week.

I meant Arthur Playfair, not Nigel. I did not know he was abroad.

G.B.S.

North British Station, Hotel,
Edinburgh.

10th Sept. 1904.

We shall be at this address for the next day or two—until further notice, in fact.

I am uneasy about the change of scene in Act II of the play. *Is* there any machinery? If not, I must set my wits to work promptly to devise means of getting over the difficulty.

G.B.S.

North British Station, Hotel,
Edinburgh.

13th Sept. 1904.

We are not coming home yet. We shall have one more try for a holiday before reheasals.

The ruling out of France is very serious. I dont know how to replace him if you are to play Keegan.

I am trying to make some rough sketches of the scenery—will send them presently. *Is* there any machinery?

G.B.S.

North British Station, Hotel,
Edinburgh.
17th Sept. 1904.

An octangular round tower is too conventionally Irish: Why build it so conscientiously? It need only be a painted profile.

Act III will be all right. No great depth is needed. There need be no space right of the house except to get in a bit of blue mountain. Entries are all down R and up L. The door in Act IV may just as well be up L as in flat.

George would of course be all right for Hodson. Asche's refusal is pretty certain; and George may be next best for Broadbent. If only Porthos Goodhart were a bit more heavenborn! Would Louis Calvert be possibile?—or is Louis the big Calvert—Mark Antony—Casca? Hallard I cant judge, only remember him as very good in Ann Leete. Dont know Agnes Thomas. Have just been asked for a part by Maud Milton. Blake Adams all right: we can find some part for him. Your mention of Thorpe is too Machiavellian. Shame!

G.B.S.

North British Station, Hotel,
Edinburgh.
18th September 1904.

If it were not for the first scene of the fourth Act, in which Nora has to make a formidable display of hysterical emotion, almost anybody could play her. But the least flatness or failure in that scene means the failure of the play: that is why I think Nina is worth trying for—Maurice is not the next resort, though he may be the last. If we have him we cannot have Charrington. Valentine as Mat: N O. I dont see S. Brough as Larry, am more inclined to Hallard, if he could be irritable enough. Old F. Cremlin, 5 Montem Road, Forest Hill, S.E. writes to me for a part. I presume he is cheap; and he would do for Corny Doyle much better than a more expensive man. I have half a mind to ask Cyril Maude to play Broadbent. J. L. Shine has a certain gentleness that would suit the priest perfectly. Doran should be more brutal. Is his brother actor enough for Doran? It will be a fearful job this casting. I dont see my way a bit.

G.B.S.

Shaw's insistence upon a good player for Nora was undoubtedly sound. The actor, Fred Cremlin, was already known to Shaw as he had produced Arms and the Man *for A. E. Drinkwater's tour of the play in 1894 and played Petkoff. Shaw afterwards wrote to John Drinkwater about this incident:*

He began his duties in the manner of a drill sergeant, with the immediate result that the actor engaged to play Nicola told him off in the most trenchant Billingsgate and shook the dust off his feet as he retired. I had to explain to Cremlin—with an eye to your father—that actors were now university men and wouldn't stand that sort of thing.

Cremlin was a player of limited range but forceful, and with vast experience; he fell into Shaw's ways and played many small parts with the Court company. The discussion about casting continues in the next five letters.

Marine Hotel, North Berwick.
21st Sept. 1904.

Your letter of Monday does not suggest anything to me that gets us much further. Ambrose Manning is most intensely un-Irish, and, like Thalberg and Stewart Headlam, has had a narrow escape of a lisp.

I considered Waring, but decided against him. One difficulty about the men who have arrived is that they wont work; and the part is a very laborious one. I am too sleepy to suggest anything myself—had a bad night and am out of sorts.

G.B.S.

Marine Hotel, North Berwick.
22nd Sept. 1904.

Dear Barker,

Your suggestion of Soutar &c for Larry have wakened me up suddenly to the common sense of the situation. The solution as to Larry is obvious. J. L. Shine must play him. The broad effect of the play will depend largely on Larry being very markedly and genuinely Irish; and Shine is that, and is also quite good enough for leading business. So propose it to him at once and get it off your mind.

Barnes is just the man for Father Dempsey. If he wants Doran, tell him I said he was not coarse enough for it—that there is always a touch of dignity about him which marks him out for the priest. So *thats* settled too. But times seem changed from the day when Jack scorned McComas at the Haymarket.

Is Dick Purdon anywhere about? He is a bad stage Irishman— a Dublin man imitating a peasant with a thoroughly false and Philistine conception of him as a vulgar person in the slumpy way of vulgarity; but he would do for Doran at a pinch. All things considered I think Blake Adams had better play Tim Haffigan.

I am utterly bothered about Matt Haffigan, who is the best of all the dialect people, and cannot be faked. Is Boucicault (Irene's husband) possible? Has he inherited any of his father's genius and has he ever been in Ireland? We want a real actor for him: a mere stuck on bit of character acting wont do: the creature must be volcanic.

I suppose Charrington still holds Bourne Cottage, Beenham, Near Reading, unless he has shot the moon. I havnt heard of him for ages. Athole Stewart was playing with him in the Doll's House lately somewhere. Athole, by the way, wants a part. He says "I have a really fine Irish brogue, my own idea, and you cant tell the difference at a distance." Now I dont want to give Charrington a part for the sake of giving him a part: thats not business. But other things being equal, I should give him anything that would fit him. I dont see where he comes in particularly here; but if Barnes refused Dempsey, he might serve.

If Athole Stewart's brogue is up to his own account of it, he might do for Patsy if we have to shift Graham Browne: he has the air of a pretty lad, which is what I want for the part.

Hendrie, if his Irish will pass, had better play Doran. If it wont, Hodson. But George is the man for Hodson if he doesnt play Broadbent. And so we are getting pretty mixed.

However, if J. L. Shine as Larry and Barnes as Dempsey will work, we have advanced a step.

I think Cremlin will do for Corney. He is an old actor with a striking resemblance to John Stuart Mill, and a great fund of conscientious and perfectly useless counsel to all sorts and conditions of theatrical enterprise.

Matt Haffigan (? Hendrie) is the difficulty.

Irene Fitzgerald suggests herself as a possible Nora. Do you know her work? Has she sufficient intestine for the emotional scene? She's too young, I think. What is the O'Malley's age?

"Sharp workmanship," unless it is authentically Irish, is rather alarming for Aunt Judy; but I take Agnes Thomas on your judgment, never having seen her to my knowledge.

I am afraid we must cut at rehearsals—according to our cloth. We shall be back before the 6th. anyhow.

G.B.S.

P.S. I dont know what Graham Browne's salary is; but I dont think any part open to him is worth what one imagines he got from Alexander in The Importance.

The part of Father Dempsey was first played by Charles Daly. J. H. Barnes played it in a later revival. He was the actor who had thrown up the part of Finch McComas in You Never Can Tell *after Shaw's reading of the play when Cyril Maude was thinking of doing it in 1896; he afterwards played the part at the Court. Dick Purdon was an Irishman who never played for Shaw. Charles Charrington never played at the Court.*

Barker was still doubtful about playing Keegan, but Shaw meant him to do it. The suggestion that Barker should make a dramatic version of George Meredith's Diana of the Crossways *for Ada Rehan is to be noted in the following two letters. It was not carried out; but six years later Barker produced a Meredith fragment.*

Marine Hotel, North Berwick.
23rd Sept. 1904.

Dear Barker,

My last letter deals with your cast. Better write to Shine at once and tell him Dempsey was a mistake—that I want him for one of the big parts. What about Louis Calvert for Broadbent? Is he grotesquely fat? A reasonable stoutness will be quite in character. In that case George can play Hodson; but if we have to choose between George and Maurice, George has worked for the new school and should have the *pas*. Lay your mind to

35

Calvert for a moment: he has the weight, and is, on the whole, the best man yet proposed, not excepting even Asche.

I dont remember Cattley, nor Williams.

Tim Haffigan must not be a real Irishman; so Blake Adams had better play him. It is a very desirable part, because the actor can get away half an hour after the curtain rises and do a turn at a music hall or at another theatre.

I think I had better wire to you about Calvert. If I knew his address I should write to him myself—at least I feel like that now. It will pass off in half an hour.

It is possible for you to play Larry and Sheeyine Keegan; and J.L. will jump at the change if you propose it. If you were an Irishman the change would hurt you more than the play. But as it is you are bound not to funk Keegan. The only real objection is the combination of management with the study and acting of a trying part; so nurse yourself all you can. Fortunately its a recreative part and not a debauching one.

Another matter. Ada Rehan is obsessed with the notion of playing Diana of The Crossways. I told her I might get someone to adapt it for her. Now you are the only playwright with anything of the quality of Meredith's style. Suppose you try your hand.

G.B.S.

Marine Hotel, North Berwick.
27th Sept. 1904.

Dear Barker,

All this about Thorpe is the utterest rot. There is no real alternative to you as Keegan; so you may make up your mind to him finally. A comfort to have *one* part settled.

Do not break finally with Graham Browne: we may have to cast him for Larry if Shine does not come off. It is the only part that would be worth his salary (what *is* his salary, by the way?). Barnes had better have his choice of Dempsey or Doran. What does he want—Broadbent? We might even be driven back on him for Matt Haffigan; but that way madness lies. Doran would be just as fat for him; so give him Doran if he will take it. If not, I suppose Wilfred Shine will do.

What about Lillah McCarthy's brother, whom I saw play

Macduff on that memorable occasion when Lillah won my heart? If he has been improving since then, he ought to be able to play Larry. If degenerating, he ought to be unable to play anything whatsoever.

Clarence has been running in my head for Matt Haffigan; but he may be quite unable to tackle an Irish part for all I know. George is so intensely English that I cannot see him in or near the part. The part is beyond Cosham, I'm afraid. He has more conscience than fire. Still, I am friendly to him.

Anything from Calvert?

There is just one possibility as to Nora that we have not discussed—Kate Rorke! She is invincibly Irish; but she is too highly civilised. On the whole, if Ellen O'Malley can rise to the fourth act, she is extraordinarily suitable in many ways; and I assume that she is a good deal cheaper than Nina or Kate. I am quite game to try her.

This letter writing is awful, I admit; and there is no chance of our getting away for a few days yet, as Charlotte is not in trim for travelling. However, as reports from my banker are comparatively favorable, and the fault is mine, why not telegraph and make me pay? It would save wear and tear to both of us.

The cutting will be awful. All the tissue seems to me to be vital: I cant get the blue pencil in without cutting an artery. However, it's got to be done.

Daly I know not. Keep him in mind for Dempsey if Barnes takes Doran.

Ada Rehan is the most ticklish of all the gold fishes: I cant imagine her commissioning anything or anybody except impulsively. But a good adaptation of Diana (which I never read) would be a marketable commodity anyhow, I think. Daly writes that she is convulsively denying that she is going to do Brassbound; but this is only newspaper report, which is at present beggaring all recorded extravagance concerning me and my plays. I will write to her and tell her that I am persuading you to take Diana in hand.

G.B.S.

Ellen O'Malley did in fact play Nora. Daniel McCarthy, Lillah McCarthy's elder brother, after his amateur stage experience had

been reading for the bar, but returned to the stage and played
many parts. He appeared as Larry in September the following
year. Shaw is not finished, however, with the casting of the Irish
play and how it should be rehearsed; he is referring to the first
reading in the following letter.

Marine Hotel, North Berwick.
30th Sep. 1904.

Dear Barker,

As to this reading, it is an odious, long and fatiguing business;
and it divides itself into two parts: one concerning Broadbent
and Larry, Keegan and Nora, and the other—Act III and Act
IV Sc 1, concerning the smaller dialect parts. This we must
bear in mind in arranging and timing the rehearsals, so as not
to have people waiting about uselessly and talking in corners.
When I wired this morning I had a notion that I might read
one day for the principals and another day the third Act and
Doran's big scene for the rest, but I suppose that will be more
trouble than it is worth, and I had better go through with the
whole thing as soon as the play is cut and cast.

Shine's absence is very unfair to the others; and I do not feel
justified in sanctioning it on my own account. The results in
McKinnel's case were disastrous, and damaged Kate Rorke more
than she knew, because Mac obliterated half her part by not
playing to it. Fortunately Nora is far less dependent on Larry
than Candida on Morell; but still I feel strongly that the dropping of a week's rehearsal by her feeder should not be sanctioned
over her head; and if it were not for the difficulty of running the
Court scheme without stretching a point or two I should say it
ought not to be sanctioned at all.

What is J.L.S's engagement; and what would he forfeit by
chucking it?

It is a question whether Graham Browne with uninterrupted
rehearsal is not better than Shine with intervals. Not that I
have ever succeeded in getting G.B. to act except in parts like
Widowers' Houses, which he did quite spontaneously, but still
I think he would pass as Larry.

The cutting still appals me. Cut all you can; and I'll presently attack it and cut all *I* can. The two excisions ought to lighten the load a bit.

G.B.S.

Marine Hotel, North Berwick, N.B.
3rd October 1904.

Granville Barker,

Do you wish to drive me mad? WHY do you keep on asking me whether I "really" wish Barnes to refuse Dempsey. I suggested him for Dempsey. I never uttered or wrote or wired a syllable to imply that there was the faintest objection to him for Dempsey if you could afford to have him for it. And here you are with a fixed idea that Barnes rankles in me. Your head is addled over the job; and you want to addle mine.

I cannot understand your clinging to George as a possible Matt Haffigan. Is he an Irishman? He seems, from all I have seen him do, to be just the very utter last man alive to touch it. Blake Adams is bad enough. I dont believe he can be Irish at all except under high pressure and false vivacity; but he is more like it than George.

If Barnes does Dempsey (I do NOT object to his doing it) Daly could, I suppose, do Corney.

I have been looking through the III act and think it is as well that we retain Shine. G.B. would not be good in the candidate scene.

The cutting bothers me fearfully. There is too much in the play. I think I shall have to cut out Keegan and Matt Haffigan chock-a-block: there are five separate tragedies in the thing besides the Broadbent comedy.

Do you fully understand that I shall be quite satisfied with Barnes as Dempsey?

I protest again and again that your Chesneys and Comptons and Couttses and so on do not exist for me. Why demand my opinion of phantasms? I never saw them. I question whether anybody ever saw them.

On reading the IV act I am more than ever impressed with the necessity of getting Nina. That scene with Larry requires great emotional play of exactly her kind. We *must* get her and

39

Dot. Tell them those are my *orders*. The booming of "How He Lied to Her Husband" (Bouchier wrote for it by return of post) ought to help us.

Barnes will do very well for Dempsey. You could not have a better man.

Our train gets to Kings Cross, if punctual, at 9. So if you look us up at 10, we shall probably be there.

G.B.S.

P.S. I assure you I have NO grudge against Barnes.

Shaw was concerned about the setting of the play as perhaps never before, and did some sketches for the sets, of which one survives. It is in colour, Act 4, scene 1, the parlour at Corney Doyle's. As carried out, the set had a door down right and another door up left, as indicated, above the fireplace, with both sofa and sideboard against the rear wall, a centre table, and with a chair before the fire.

While all this was going on the Vedrenne-Barker Matinees were announced to start at the Court Theatre on 18 October. Tuesdays. Thursdays and Fridays were the days chosen so as not to conflict with the regular theatre matinee days, Wednesdays and Saturdays. This arrangement made it possible for actors otherwise engaged to take part in them.

The first piece was the Hippolytus of Euripides in Dr. Gilbert Murray's version, which Barker had produced for the New Century Theatre at the Lyric Theatre on the previous 24 May. In this memorable Court production, Ben Webster played Hippolytus, Edyth Olive Phaedra, and Barker the Messenger. Barker's delivery of the messenger's speech was highly praised. A. B. Walkley said that "the Phèdre of Miss Edyth Olive is by no means unworthy to compare with the Phèdre of Mme. Bernhardt." Writing to Gilbert Murray Barker said of the play, "It has been good and satisfying work to throw oneself at a big block of marble to chip, instead of putty as most plays are." An announcement in the programme read:

"As the three minutes' interval in the middle of the play presents no break in the action, it is felt that the appearance of the performers is (at that time) undesirable."

As the desire of the new management was to get away from plays that were, as Shaw said, "a tailor's advertisement making sentimental remarks to a milliner's advertisement in the middle of an upholsterer's and decorator's advertisement," there could have been no more significant opening than this Greek master-piece. Dr. Gilbert Murray, who comes of a distinguished Austral-ian family, was at that time Professor of Greek at Oxford Uni-versity; he was on the committee of the Stage Society, and a close friend of William Archer and Bernard Shaw. In his transla-tions of the Greek classic dramatists he used verse, but aimed to create living drama out of the Greek originals. His versions were adversely criticised because his metres were his own; but his ob-ject was to get the verse spoken as living speech, and, while being true to the spirit and form of the drama, to eliminate as far as possible archaic elements.

John Bull's Other Island was produced on 1 November 1904, and allowed the usual six matinees. It was an immediate success. The theatre was packed. It was hoped to have the presence of the Prime Minister, A. J. Balfour, at the first performance, but he could not come. When he did see the play, on 10 November, Mrs. Sidney Webb being his hostess, Balfour was delighted, and came again, bringing the leader of the Opposition with him, Campbell-Bannerman, and later, on a third visit, H. H. Asquith. A letter written by Shaw to an actress friend who had asked him for stalls at the first performance is worth adding to the collection: it indicates not only one great demand for seats, but Shaw's aversion to granting free seats to anyone:

No words can express the impossibility of my getting 3 stalls for tomorrow. Tree has had to *buy* a box, Alexander having secured stalls by planking down solid gold. I have had to buy a stall for my mother for the second performance; and I should have surrendered my box if I had not promised to hide a son of Sir William Harcourt in it, as he cannot yet appear publicly in a theatre.

As I know that some authors practically reserve the whole reserved part of the house for invitations at first performances, I must explain that I do the opposite and never touch the front of the house. Except for the author's box at the first performance every seat I get is paid for; so that I am in a much worse position than you; you can always command seats by professional courtesy when seats are going; but as I expect the management to stick strictly to its bargain with me, I am bound to stick strictly to my bargain with it—at all events I make it a rule to do so. Otherwise I should joyfully give you all the stalls in the house and throw in the front row of the balcony as well, merely for the pleasure of seeing you.

But may I gently reproach you for making such a demand at the last moment? Even the most desperate ventures manage to fill up the first house some days before the curtain goes up. And if they didn't they would have to pretend that they did.

"The play is not all rot," gasped Walkley *in* The Times, *bewildered by its overwhelming flood of humorous rhetoric, though he admitted that it went beyond mere "brilliancy," concluding his review by saying that it is, "of course, not a play but a thoroughly characteristic 'Shavian' entertainment."*

William Archer wrote, "Mr. Shaw has done nothing more original—nothing, to my thinking, more delightful." Max Beerbohm declared, "Broadbent, in all the various relations of life, is certainly Mr. Shaw's masterpiece of observation and satire." Desmond MacCarthy said that the interest of the play "lies solely in the presentation of character and in the contrast between temperaments." He added with emphasis that "the performance itself was one of the best ever given in London," a tribute to Shaw as producer. E. F. Spence complained in The Sketch *of "its excessive length and total lack of form." And there was a fault-finding notice in the* Daily Telegraph, *which grudgingly combined blame and praise:*

". . . the fact is that whether owing to the folly of the author's cleverness or the cleverness of his folly, the 'new and unpublished play' is anything but effective . . .There is a most original love scene . . . purple patches abound . . . graceful and tender little scenes and passages are sandwiched between great hunks of bombastic frivolity . . . What such a piece should be called, whether political tract, imaginative fantasia, rollicking farce, or pyrotechnic display, it would tax the human ingenuity to deter-

mine. The one thing that is certain is that it is not a play. 'It's all tommy rot,' cries one character . . . Whatever else Mr. Shaw may do, he certainly makes us despair. We laugh with a wry face at pessimism grinning behind a comic mask. There is nothing genial or generous or human in Mr. Shaw's mirth. In this play, which was no play, and never apparently intended to be one, there were several opportunities for good acting . . . We cannot say . . . that the make-up of the characters was in every case a success . . . and the piece as a whole was insufficiently rehearsed."

The length of play was indeed a problem. After cutting, it played from 2.30 to 6. Barker was thinking of evening perform-ances and was lamenting its too-late finish. The play was in fact severely cut, and the printed text is part only of what was orig-inally written; even that was cut; no less than 50 lines from Broadbent and Tim Haffigan's opening conversation in Act 1, and approximately 144 lines from the discussion between Broad-bent and Larry later in the same act, and in the last scene of Act IV, 159 lines, or thereabouts, partly from Broadbent, but mostly from Keegan. At the Court there was not much further cutting, but when the play came to be done later there was more cutting here and there. This was unusual in Shaw's plays, though in the standard edition of his work he made revisions of the text in this and a number of other plays, arising, he said, out of experience in performance. Shaw's objection to the cutting of his plays was not to the mere cutting but to managements or actors cutting to suit their own interpretation of play or characters irrespective of the playwright's intentions. Shaw comments sarcastically on Barker's cutting. "Lady Mary" was the wife of Gilbert Murray.

The six matinees were completed on 11 November and he writes one week later:

The Old House, Harmer Green, Welwyn.
6th December 1904.

Your labors—heroic, I gratefully admit—are conclusive. With regard to all that part of the play which you took part in yourself for six performances, you find that it can't be cut except in mere desperation, to shorten the last scene.

As to the rest, you cut it as Irving cut Lear: that is, cut wherever you can make a skip and a clean joint. Nora fades ineffectively from the stage with a little gasp like the last flicker of a burnt-out candle. Broadbent's laughs are cut out (obviously under the influence of Lady Mary) because they encourage him in buffoonery; but I grieve to say that Keegan's solemnities are not cut out on the far more serious ground that they encourage him in slow preaching. You will be stupended at my meanness in this obvious and cheap retort; but if you send the play round to the rest of the cast and ask them to cut it, they will all do the same thing in perfectly good faith. Playfair, for instance, wont cut his reason for being a Home Ruler, one of the most quoted and penetrating passages in the play on the superficial political side. Broadbent wont cut his naturalization reductio-ad-abandum of Gladstonian pro-Irishism. Nora wont cut her exit—perhaps the best exit in the play. But they will skip and join gaily in the passages that did not come home to themselves; and the total result will be a very brief play indeed. Irving got Lear down to one third of its length. Result: an unbearably tedious failure, because the characters became mere shells. The mechanical part of them walked and stalked; their souls and the air of ancient Britain had fled. If he had played the original from 6 to 12 word for word, or smartened his own business and played it from 7.30 to 11.30, the people would have been very weary; but they'd have been fascinated and talked about it for a week after so that everybody they talked to *must* have gone to it. Now you want to do the same thing to John Bull, partly because you want to save time at any cost, but partly because you have as much taste for Ireland as Irving has for Shakespear, and some sound natural dislike into the bargain.

There is only one way out of the difficulty; and that is to rewrite the play as a West End theatre piece. To this there are two objections: first, that I dont want to sacrifice my aim to the box office, and, second, that I could write a new play in the time. It would be much more sensible to announce a Shaw festival, and play the piece at its full original length, two acts after lunch and two after dinner.

No: there's nothing to be done but either drop the play—which, after all, has served its turn pretty well—or else play it as before from 2.30 to 6 (or whatever it was) and from 8 to 11.30 if you hamper yourself with an evening performance. But better let it go altogether; for the difficulty of getting the cast together again will be considerable—insuperable if you play at night, probably.

I am sorry to be pigheaded; but right is necessarily pigheaded. Your first act (or scene) in Cork, with Broadbent already in tweeds on Irish soil, would be about ten minutes longer than the existing first act, and would do its work worse. It's no use: you cant get round the central immovable fact that there are too many life histories in John Bull to be lived in two hours and a quarter. The theme is a huge one; and it cant be cut down to Court size. Almost all the misfires which have already occurred have been caused by the omissions: a cut play is always a long one. Bow, therefore, hardily to Fate, and waste no more time over a hopeless job.

Miss Tita, quite uncrushed—nay, stimulated by being called a flouncing rhapsodist and a dozen other names; challenged also to name any *human* thing she can do; now without the smallest hint from me, asks to be allowed to study Gloria. The more I think of this, the more I feel disposed to make a virtue of Tita's difference from the leading lady type (an Italian prima donna type essentially) and try whether we cannot educate the public a little in that direction. It's rather a case of Rebecca or Rowena; and as you violently object to Rebecca, you had better give Rowena a chance. After all Tita has a personality of an ardent kind; and it is just this personality that rules her, whereas if we had a scrap of originality it would rule her in. Mrs. Theodore Wright and Tita would make Y.N.C.T. a perfectly new thing. It has always seemed merely a farce written round a waiter. It ought to be a very serious comedy, dancing gaily to a happy ending round the grim-earnest of Mrs. Clandon's marriage and her XIX century George-Eliotism. You are at present such an old professional that you are much more Philistine than Vedrenne; and unless you make haste to become as a little child again, you will have musical comedy on at the Court before the end of 1905. No time for more. I dont think we shall come up to Adelphi until Friday morning.

G. Bernard Shaw.

Tita Brand, mentioned in the above letter, had been to Shaw to ask him for a part. She had previously appeared on the Court stage as the Leader of the Chorus in Hippolytus; *she was the daughter of Marie Brema. He wrote her a characteristic letter:*

10, Adelphi Terrace, W.C.
30th Nov. 1904.

My dear Miss Tita,

You are a most unreasonable and exacting young lady. I paid you the highest compliment on your recital; but because there was a crumple in one or two of the roseleaves you have treated me ever since as Shelley treated the reviewers of Keats.

And now you want a part in one of my plays! Am I Milton, or Aeschylus, to find parts for a great flouncing, superheroic rhapsodist like you? Can I hang you on the wall in Candida instead of Titian's Assumption? Is Sloane Square Bayreuth? are my heroines Frickas or Kundrys or Ortruds? Conceive Barker's feeling if I propose that you should play a mere real woman and marry a mere real trumpery man at the end of the play instead of going bang up to Olympus like Artemis in Hippolytus! It is a grand thing to be like one of Michelangelo's sybils; but it makes difficulties when modern comedies have to be cast.

I really don't know what to say to you. Short of boiling you for several days I don't know how you could be brought within practical limits; and your mother would probably object to that.

Come! what part do you want to play? I should like to try you; for nobody knows what can or cannot be done with your sort of talent and personality on the modern stage. But it is difficult to propose experiments, however interesting to the author, with Vedrenne's and Barker's money. I am quite friendly, and more appreciative than you yourself dare be; but I dont know what to do with you. Tell me your own views.

Yours faithfully,

G. Bernard Shaw.

After the actress was given the part of Gloria in You Never Can Tell *there arose some difficulty because she wanted to play Desdemona in a production of* Othello *by Hubert Carter at another theatre. At first Shaw was adamant; "I am off to look for another Gloria," he wrote in exasperation. But when the play was done the following 2 May, she was the first Gloria on the Court Theatre stage.*

To recover from the failure of the Housman-Barker Prunella, *which followed at Christmas,* John Bull's Other Island, *was put on for nine matinees, and a command performance took place on 11 March 1905, in the evening, for His Majesty King Edward VII. Royal recognition thus set the seal on the management, but no risk was taken with regular evening performances until 1 May when the play was given a three weeks' run with Lillah McCarthy making her first appearance at the Court in the part of Nora. Thereafter, evening performances became the rule, in addition to the matinees.*

Before this there was a triple bill for nine matinees starting on 28 February consisting of W. B. Yeats' The Pot of Broth, *Arthur Schnitzler's* In The Hospital, *and Bernard Shaw's* How He Lied to Her Husband. *Barker produced the first and second, and played the Lover in the third. Shaw gives vigorous expression to what he thought of the performance in the following letter.*

The Old House, Harmer Green, Welwyn.
1st March 1905.

Dear Barker,

The complaint of the classic Crummles against the low buffoonery of the comic countrymen is eternal and eternally in vain.

You and Gertrude act like two very clever and accomplished people in that play; but Poulton does not act. He is a force of Nature, enormous, irresistible, not knowing what he does. Let him stand on his head if he likes. He is fascinating, obsessing: he raises the thing to a world epic. Respect him; worship him; let him alone. Take off your hat when his eyes—Oh, those eyes!—blaze on you.

The end of the play will never go, because the audience shriek so violently at the tumbling about the floor that they are exhausted. I foresaw this: it doesnt matter.

You did Candida, Candida, Candida the wrong way. Miss Kingston mustnt open the door when she wants the vinegar and brown paper. She overacts "no, it's no use: I've begun to think of you as Mr. Upjohn &c" *Dont* change the coat: Walkley be blowed! For the rest it's all right and will come righter. You both do not need any compliments over an idiotic farce, do you? Now for Euripedes! Miss Brema will open at the end of March to appease me.

G.B.S.

These matinees of three short plays were not a success, and Shaw wrote to Vedrenne on 23 March:

As the play proved worthless and you did your best for it I will not aggravate its failure by asking royalties, which I hereby formally waive, forego and disclaim.

When the three weeks' run of the Irish play ended, Candida *followed it in the evening bill for another three weeks, with Barker as Eugene.*

Then the long-awaited Man and Superman *entered upon its twelve matinees on 23 May, following two Stage Society performances. The play had been published the year before the Vedrenne-Barker management with a preface in the form of a long letter to A. B. Walkley, and a "Revolutionist's Handbook" at the end, so that it was well known. The performances of Barker as Jack Tanner and Lillah McCarthy as Ann Whitefield are never likely to be excelled. The* Globe *came out with the statement:*

"With the production, yesterday afternoon, of Man and Superman, *against the morality of which nothing whatever is to be urged, Mr. Shaw takes definitely his place among the actable and the acted."*

The candid Daily Telegraph *critic declared:*

"Of course, the title has little or nothing to do with the play. . . . Nor, indeed, is there a play at all. . . . It is a comedy of a sort, a comedy that consists of brilliant utterances, of contrasted characters, of episodes which follow one another and are not indissolubly connected in a plot, of fragments of philosophy, or rather social ethics, which meet and cancel each other . . . And now having delivered ourselves of these obvious and platitudinous remarks—which, after all, only amount to the assertion that we have been witnessing a play of Bernard Shaw's—let us

frankly admit that it is one of the most amusing pieces of work which even the Court Theatre has ever put upon the stage. . . . These are admirably drawn characters. . . . . Whatever else Mr. Shaw may do, he enables our actors and actresses to do themselves abundant justice, and that is no slight book."

In Desmond MacCarthy's judgement, "The whole performance was extraordinarily good . . . all reached that pitch of excellence in their parts which makes a living person start up before the mind's eye afterwards, whenever the name of the character is mentioned."

When Candida *finished,* You Never Can Tell *succeeded it in the evening bill on 12 June for three weeks, with the same cast as for the matinees. The theatre was closed the greater part of July and throughout August. There is a gap in the correspondence not because Shaw ceased to write, but Barker did not, unfortunately, preserve the letters.*

Shaw was taken away by Charlotte on holiday to Ireland for the first time in twenty-nine years. The violent letter to Ellen Terry referred to in the following letter seems not to have been preserved. He had promised the name part in his new play Major Barbara *to Ada Rehan, who had met with an accident and did not expect to be well by 28 November when the play was to open. It was performed on that date but not with Miss Rehan. Barker was to play the Greek professor. Tyler was an American manager. Eleanor is Ellen Terry, and* Captain Brassbound *was getting near to production. Shaw's idea of including* Peer Gynt *in the programme appears in the correspondence for the first time. He never dropped the idea.*

Derry, Rosscarbery, Co. Cork.
3rd August 1905.

Dear Barker,

The situation, as I have been only too well aware, is a very serious one. I have written to Lady Barrington to ask whether Miss Rehan can take up Ellen Terry's dates; and I have written very violently to Ellen explaining the position she has landed me in. I told Vedrenne to put Brassbound out of his head for another year, instead of which he read the play, and instantly

49

felt that his whole future was staked on it. You see, when that poor lady was suddenly knocked down and gave up the part with a sense that it was giving up the stage and making an end, I sent her word to get well, and the play should wait as long as she liked, she being in want of that sort of medicine just then. I cannot go back on that at the first temptation; so unless Miss Rehan now cries off for some reason beyond the sense of obligation that led her to release the play before, I must give her time to recover.

I have just wired you Tyler's cablegram (also Vedrenne) from which you will see that Eleanor, with my vivid account of the Tyler-Vedrenne snorting match in her hand, lost no time in plunging Tyler into a passion of exculpation and protestations. The explosion occurred at Sandy Hook I imagine; or else the ship simply flew across the Atlantic. I am now writing to Tyler to say that I want Miss R. here for the 28th Novr; and if that be possible there is a chance of my getting her. But it may not be possible; and then I think Major Barbara will have to slide, and the Court to put on a pantomime. It is all very well to say that there are others. My answer is—Name! Name! Of course, a substitution is physically possible: Marie Tempest or Ethel Irving can act Barbara just as Tully can act Cusins. But if you want the higher Shaw drama you must take the higher chances. I am giving the public a very stiff dose of lecturing in the style of the last scene of John Bull; and nothing short of a cast of geniuses will be of the slightest use. You—poor devil— have to play with Calvert all through, play at him, play on him, play round him, spout Euripedes (The Bacchae) to him by the page, play Puck to his Mephistopheles in an unheard of manner; and what it will all be like, heaven itself doesn't know. We may have to wait ten years to get the conditions; or we may have luck and get them in November. But in any case we must consider Barbara is a possibility only and be prepared with an understudy.

I havent time for any more today—must close.

G.B.S.

P.S. I strenuously approve of a Brieux or Ibsen for the 2nd set of matinees. Why not Peer Gynt? Quite feasible.

Shaw is discussing the casting of Major Barbara *and* Captain Brassbound's Conversion. *The two R's are Annie Russell and Ada Rehan for the first play. Eleanor, as before, means Ellen Terry. Lady B. is Lady Barrington. What Louis Calvert thought of Undershaft he has left on record; he considered it unlearnable and unplayable, yet he made a great success of it. Shaw was always anxious that Barker should do* Peer Gynt. *His high opinion of* Mrs. Warren's Profession *is again evident.*

Derry, Rosscarbery, Co. Cork.
(Until October)
7-8-05.

All this I have already carefully set out in my mind; but the issue is still on the lap of the gods. We are all right as to the casts, apart from Barbara and Lady Cicely; so that we can wait until we get something definite about the two Rs. I have written to Tyler to say that I want Eleanor in November for various staggering reasons, and that I want her cheap, as nobody but the author is going to go into this thing for money. I have written to Lady B. and to Ellen; and none of them have yet replied. None of the letters are of a nature to be disregarded.

I do not think Widowers' Houses would go well with Hannele; they are in rather clashing keys, and are both steeped in poverty. And I havent thought of anything else. The last moment has not yet come; so stick to the Voyseys and dont worry about me: I am alive to the situation.

I rather wonder what Calvert will say to the length and intellectual complexity of Undershaft. I wrote to him to learn the trombone for the S. A. procession; but he has not answered.

If Vedrenne would care to try Redford again with Mrs. Warren at any time I will find the 2 guineas.

G.B.S.

A postcard from the same place three days later gives Barker important news:

51

Derry, Rosscarbery, Co. Cork.
10 August 1905.

You have probably heard by this time that I have given the word to engage Ellen for Brassbound; but as Tyler's letter is due now I had better wait for it before I cable, to save confusion. No use trying to rush him until I know what he has to say.

G.B.S.

Shaw dearly wanted Miss Ada Rehan for the name part in Major Barbara, *but owing to her accident she had to give up the idea. For "the higher Shaw drama . . . nothing short of a cast of geniuses will be of the slightest use," he wrote to Barker. There was constant trouble with Louis Calvert, who jibbed at Undershaft's long speeches, longer and more numerous than those of Broadbent, and, with other difficulties, the possibility of* Major Barbara *diminished for their date of 28 November. Shaw had told Professor Gilbert Murray that he was writing a play called* Murray's Mother-in-Law, *for Lady Britomart was modelled on Murray's mother-in-law, the Countess of Carlisle. This was a joke, but it was first intended to call it* Andrew Undershaft's Profession, *which would have been a huge mistake. Cusins the Greek professor had Professor Murray as his original and when Shaw asked Murray if he minded being described as a foundling he replied, "Not in the least," but he wrote to Granville Barker on 11 August: "Tell G.B.S. that I try to be a Christian, and can stand a good deal, as such. But, if people call me Adolphus, they do so at their peril—Moses, if you like, or even Ferdinand. But not Adolphus."*

On 11 September there was a welcome re-opening of the theatre with John Bull's Other Island, *Miss McCarthy's brother, Daniel, playing Larry, Edmund Gwenn Hodson, and there were a few other changes. A new dramatist was also introduced to London in St. John Hankin, whose comedy* The Return of the Prodigal *was given six matinees starting on 26 September.*

Shaw was still actively casting Major Barbara. *In the next letter, Nora Greenlaw had played the part of Privacy in the first production of* Prunella *and did understudying; Gwenn is Edmund Gwenn, of course and played Belton; Snobby was played by Arthur Laceby; Mrs. Baines was played by Edith Wynne-Matthison. Shaw went to the Salvation Army's Festival at the Albert Hall, and joined heartily in the singing. The Army liked him. Barker was taking up photography.*

Derry, Rosscarbery, Co. Cork.
28th September 1905.

Barker, Barker,

How long have you known this about Nora Greenlaw? This is the first I heard of it.

The difficulty about Snobby is that you have simply no sense of character. Unless I can get Cremlin and Yorke fitted with the right sort of Snobby we shall get the usual stock-company ensemble with no character at all in it. Of course Gwenn can play a thief. He can also play the Emperor of China. An actor is an actor and a part is only a part when all's said. Drinkwater is as much like Snobby as Falstaff is like Perolles—that much and no more. Farren Soutar could play Snobby. Yorke Stephens could *look* Snobby. You could play Snobby. I want a slim, *louche,* servant-girl-bigamist, half-handsome sort of rascal, *not* a costermonger, *not* an Artful Dodger, not anything like Gwenn. Page is far nearer the mark; but he has not the slick fluency for it. A man in the very least slow or stiff wont do. Cheeseman must be at least 80: he played Toole's parts on tour when I was thirteen. Field, Rigby and Smith are mere inventions, having no existence outside your book. Shine is too Irish. What about George? He can be fluent when he likes.

Mrs. Baines is a poor part for Geraldine Oliffe; but her voice is rather right for it; and I gather that she would take anything now. There is a Miss K. M. Robinson, 37 Adair House, Chelsea, who struck me as rather possible for middle-aged character parts. If she asks to see you, you might have a look at her; she might at all events understudy Rummy and Mrs. Baines, and even play Mrs. Baines if Geraldine is not available.

I shall be in London midday to some time on Tuesday. I want to attend the Salvation Festival at the Albert Hall on Monday.

53

The photographs are very like my Mediterranean ones. Tell them next time to make your prints on matt folio: the cost is the same; and they are not so tiring. I return the prints &c herein.

G.B.S.

On 23 October, Man and Superman *replaced* John Bull's Other Island *in the evening bill, and on 7 November, Barker's play* The Voysey Inheritance *was given its first performance, the first of six matinees. It aroused great interest, because both it and its performance, despite the charge of over-intellectuality, were so much alive. Shaw's comments are not available. The completion of* Major Barbara *was still occupying him. He had written to Vedrenne on 17 September:*

I have not looked at Major Barbara since the 8th and am in a condition of sullen desperation concerning it.

At last, however, its production was in hand and the performance actually came off on 28 November, the first of the usual six matinees, with the popular Annie Russell in the name part, Louis Calvert as Undershaft, and Granville Barker as Cusins. Notwithstanding Calvert's trouble with the length of his part, he had found that under Shaw's coaching, which caused him to turn his back on all his experience as an artist, he could well nigh reach perfection. He was not, however, a completely perfect Undershaft, for in the last act his impatience was manifest. The play was received with mingled delight and bewildered exasperation by an audience that included the Prime Minister, A. J. Balfour. Shaw called it bluntly "a discussion," and the extreme garrulity of the dramatist, as Walkley put it, caused the exasperation no less than the bewilderment. When Undershaft starts talking he goes on until his hearers are approaching exhaustion. However, the theme of the play, and the attractive Salvation Army heroine, guaranteed its success. At the first performance uniformed Salvation Army Officers were present among the intelligentzia of London. Shaw took immense pains to get his Salvation Army material correct and not to hurt the feelings of the Army. When he gave evidence before the Joint Select Committee on the

Censorship in 1909, Barker said that the Examiner of Plays had sent for him and had to be assured that the Salvation Army had no objection before he would license the play. In fact, Shaw attended meetings and was welcomed by the Army, which looked upon him as providing good publicity and lent the uniforms for the production. The theatre as such was of course rigidly taboo to the Army, but it was ready to enter hell to pluck souls from burning.

Shaw wrote in indignation to the Standard protesting against its critic's reference to the Salvation Army's "ill-tuned bands," saying he had "never heard a S.A. band that deserved your critic's reproach." He went on:

"May I take this opportunity to ask the public not to repeat the burst of applause with which they saluted Mr. Granville Barker's spirited performance on the big drum on Tuesday? Mr. Barker has no proper sense of the degradation of playing it, as one critic, not the Standard's had said; in fact his delight in the instrument has seriously interfered with the rehearsals, and may, if encouraged, lead to his abandoning the stage for the orchestra, and thereby robbing me of an actor with whom I cannot dispense, and a playwright whose works bid fair to enable the Court Theatre to dispense with me."

After the six matinees, with the theatre remaining empty over Christmas, while a number of new players were being rehearsed, there was a re-opening on 1 January 1906 with Major Barbara in the evening bill "for six weeks only."

As the letters show, the production of Captain Brassbound's Conversion was being actively prepared, for at last Ellen Terry was to play the part. In the following letter, C. L. Delph had played Lady Britomart's butler in Major Barbara; he played Redbrook in Captain Brassbound. James Carew, an American actor who first appeared on the London stage that year, had played Hector Malone in Man and Superman; he played Captain Kearney in Captain Brassbound. He afterwards accompanied Ellen Terry to America in the spring of 1906 when she went on tour under the direction of Charles Frohman, with this and other plays, and they were married at Pittsburg on 22 March 1907.

William Heinemann was a publisher who specialized in plays, and took on the publication of Ibsen's plays. Constable published Shaw's plays on commisison.

Edstaston. Wem.
20th Dec. 1905.

Dear Barker,

Your scene man may wobble idle this Xmas. I shall not be ready for him. I got four urgent letters this morning all demanding something representing a day's work by Thursday.

If Delph has nerve enough to act, I dont doubt that he will be distinguished enough.

I am serious about Carew: he would be dull in the way you suggest; but the effect might be screaming, and would be fresh anyhow. He could also understudy Brassbound, if he would; and you could understudy Kearney in an emergency.

The Heinemann project is ganz und gar out of the question as far as I am concerned. The colossal calm with which you propose, as an incident to a minor front arrangement, that I should change my publisher, bereaves me of breath. It would be almost as convenient as marrying you to Lillah to keep Ann in the family. Why not approach Constable?

Vedrenne wires call for 2 on the 28th. I may not arrive in time: in that case, dont wait for me.

G.B.S.

10, Adelphi Terrace, W.C.
8th Jan. 1906.

Dear H.G.B.

Will you please ask Stier whether the enclosed notation of the chanty in Brassbound is correct, and if not, to alter it for me. That done, will some kind friend add the words, which I totally forget.

Thursday morning or afternoon, or Friday morning—*not* afternoon—will suit me for the reading of the Phil. I cannot go to the show today, as the Freie Volkbuhne of Berlin have calmly announced *8* piratical performances of Widowers' Houses, and I must draw up, swear and send off an elaborate affidavit by to-night's post to stop them.

Yr ever,

G.B.S.

Theodore Stier referred to in the above letter was the con-ductor of the Court Theatre orchestra. He was an admirable musician, who later became musical director for Pavlova for fif-teen years. "Phil" means The Philanderer. *The Shaws had just moved to the Old Rectory, Ayot St. Lawrence, and St. John Hankin's comedy,* The Cassalis Engagement *was performed by the Stage Society on 10 February.*

Ayot St. Lawrence, Welwyn Herts.
12th Feb. 1906.

We are down here until Thursday afternoon.

Hankin has wiped our eyes very dry with Cassilis, which would not have a dull moment in it if the second act were com-petently played.

Does your good news mean that the deed of darkness and sanguinary ruffianism has been done, or only that the move has been successful?

The following is written on a card and though bearing the Harmer Green address, the writer was using old stationary. F.K. is Frederick Kerr playing Mr. Voysey in the revival of Barker's play which took place on this date.

Harmer Green, Welwyn
12th Feb. 1906.

F.K. had a good idea about Voysey having a flower in his coat. I think something could be done at the end of the first act with a flower and a looking glass. I see the old gentleman throwing the grand disclosure off his chest and titivating himself for a jolly day—taking the flower out of a glass of water and sticking it in his buttonhole—looking at himself in the mirror and blossoming generally after his little coup de theatre in contrast to the wilted Edward. It all fits in so well—the bit of pathos, and

57

the final "Dont brood, Edward, dont brood" which should be extremely cocky.

And dont suppress your people too much. Remember the infernal accoustics of the theatre.

V.D. has set Ellen on to me worse than ever by saying that he is not going to the provinces. Implore him to be discreet; these people desolate my existence.

G.B.S.

Barker was taking an active part in the rehearsals of Captain Brassbound's Conversion, *Shaw looking on and advising him. The chanties were provided by John Masefield in the nick of time.*

10, Adelphi Terrace, W.C.
14th March 1906.

Dear Barker,

I did not do anything about the chanty. We should have a special rehearsal of extras for it if we attempt it: it is impossible to stop a rehearsal for it. Unless they pick it up very easily it wont be worth the trouble.

Do not let Ellen repeat any scene. When she gets through she always wants to do it over and over again until it is right. There are two fatal objections. 1. She always goes to pieces the second time and discourages and demoralizes herself more and more every time. 2. She has just strength to get through the play once without tiring herself and before lunch; and the repetition of a scene means a corresponding omission at the end. Go straight through and dont let them stop for anything. In any case the policy of sticking at it until we get it is a vulgar folly. Let them take their failure and the shame of it home and they will think about it and pull it off next time.

Do not make Casson *play out*. It spoils the part completely and anticipates the Cadi, who plays out all the time. The contrast between the immovably dignified and self contained Sidi and the rumbustious blethering Cadi cannot be too marked. If there is the slightest self assertion in the line "Brassbound: I am in my own house and among mine own people. *I* am the Sultan here," the effect is utterly lost. It should be as the voice of God.

Delph is hopelessly bothered and puzzled by the business of taking off Sir Howard; and no wonder, as the dialogue is quite wrong for the new business. Possibly it may help to have more words for Sir Howard—for instance, "You will be laid by the heels yet, my friend (they seize him) You have no right to lay your hands on me, sir. You are breaking the law. You are committing an assault. I will let you know that you cannot outrage me with impunity. Your captain is a scoundrel who is getting you and himself into trouble. I will not stand &c &c &c &c &c." Meanwhile Johnson can say "All right, sir, all right: take it easy: nobody's offering to hurt you: better leave the cap'n to himself: no offence: steady on: come along, sir." Redbrook can say Tut tut &c as in the book. I think if they all talk themselves off the stage together without bothering about Lady Cicely, it will not only be more natural, but she may quite easily be reassured by the men's talk that they will not hurt him. If we try the other Delph will botch it.

Kerr thinks the meeting too slow, as he works himself up a good deal over it. You might mention to him beforehand that the effect is more convincing when they are obviously half hearted and all the vigor is on his side. Say I watched it carefully today and came to that conclusion.

Do let us have the Court stage and the scenery on Saturday as well as on Monday. Remember how the scenery in John Bull knocked Calvert to pieces—Blunt has no saddles worth talking about; so we must do with a couple of bales.

G.B.S.

At last Captain Brassbound's Conversion *had its six matinees, starting on 20 March, with Ellen Terry in the part written for her. The cast was entirely different from that of the Stage Society's production more than five years earlier. Desmond MacCarthy, who admired the play, considered the performance "below the usual mark and not so good as the Stage Society's." The cast did not "pull the play together" and there was an "absence of sureness" in Miss Terry's acting. Indeed, the production was far from*

59

being a success, and Ellen Terry was not the draw she was ex-
pected to be. In fact, every one was altogether too self-conscious,
and the extreme trouble taken with it was unrewarded. Shaw had
written to Ellen Terry on the previous 17 August when her play-
ing in it had been settled:

"I am looking forward with malicious glee to the rehearsals. I
shall have my revenge then. I will not leave a rag, not a wink, not
a flipperty top of that tiresome Ellen Terry who would not do my
play."

The actress found him considerate and charming. He allowed
her to make the play her own, and gave her very favourable
terms when later she went on tour with it.

After two Greek plays, Captain Brassbound's Conversion went
into the evening bill for twelve weeks from 16 April. During
this run the theatre was closed for one night—the day before
Ellen Terry's jubilee. On the actual date, Saturday 28 April,
a special programme was presented to each member of the audi-
ence containing the autographs of the manager, author, all the
cast, the business manager, stage director, box office keeper, and
musical director. On 5 May she wrote to "Dearest G.B.S." asking
him to come and see the play:

"We are nearly all of us going astray one way or another ... I
don't do it 'on purpose' but I'm sure to have gone wrong, and
should be tremendously obliged by corrections from you, if you
will spare the time."

Later this month there was some talk of Madge McIntosh
having to take over the part of Lady Cecily and on 16 May
Shaw wrote to Vedrenne at some length, for he was much dis-
turbed by the poor business:

We ought to seize the opportunity to announce Miss McIntosh's
appearance as Lady C. Even if it emptied the house, the statistical
information would be well worth the loss: in fact, I'll bear half of
it willingly ... The returns are not at all satisfactory. The average

house for the matinees was £149:15:9. The average house in the evening up to the end of last week was £92.7.6., say £85. for the management, £6.18.0 for the author and £23:11:0 for the leading lady. Net result probably about £2:10:0 apiece for V. & B. to live on and pile up future capital for the new theatre. This does not seem to me to be good enough to maintain three flats in London and quarters in the Tyrol. All our real successes—John Bull and Superman to wit—have been with modest and youthful casts; and the question is, are we throwing away £170. a week? Or to put it another way, will a fashionable leading lady in DsD [Doctor's Dilemma] draw the difference between her salary and Miss Lambourne's. However, I am bound to say that I don't think the lukewarmness of the C.P. [Court Public] towards Brassbound is Miss Terry's fault—as far as the acting and not the play itself is in fault. For some reason, Drinkwater is not amusing in the first act, and Brassbound is not thrilling in the second. It may be my fault; but at all events it is not Miss Terry's; and it breaks Lady C's back rather. Sometimes I think the play is no good. Sometimes I wonder whether the cast just misses the mark. I must have another look at it soon.

There is, of course, a structural fault in the play, and Shaw was right to have doubts about it. He had written it for Ellen and he had no doubts about her. What he thought is indicated in a letter to J. Forbes-Robertson more than eighteen months later when Ellen Terry was touring with the play and he saw it at the Grand Theatre, Fulham:

Her whole company were blind and mad with nightly repetition of their wretched parts . . . but Ellen herself was magnificent. She had actually become Lady Cecily. She no longer hampers herself as she did at the Court by trying to remember my lines: she simply lives through Lady Cecily's adventures and says whatever comes into her head, which by the way is now much better than what I wrote.

He was also inveighing against the effect of the long run and warning Forbes-Robertson himself who was touring with Caesar and Cleopatra.

On 24 April 1906 Lillah McCarthy and Granville Barker were married at the registry office in Henrietta Street, Strand, in the presence of her father and Barker's solicitor Matthews. No one else was there but the registrar. At the same registry office, Bernard Shaw had been married in 1898. The couple left for Paris where they were met by Shaw, who was being sculptured by Rodin; they went out to the sculptor's house for luncheon, then to Germany and to the Tyrol. Barker wrote to Shaw about a performance of Caesar and Cleopatra *they had seen in Berlin, produced by Reinhardt. The play the Shaws saw at the Théâtre Antoine was Ibsen's* The Wild Duck.

Hotel Palais d'Orsay. Paris.
7th May 1906.

My dear Barker,

May the soul of Reinhardt scream through all eternity in boiling brimstone! The cut explains everything. It is that first scene of the 4th act that effects the modulation of the play into the serious key of the murder scene. I have written to Trebitsch about it. I do not see how the end of the 2nd act explains itself without the burning of the library.

We went to the Antoine the night before the revolution, and found it calmly closed—no reason alleged—got our money back. Went on with Trebitsch to the Grand Guignol and saw four out of five short plays, all fairly amusing, especially a farce with a guillotine in it. On the first of May Paris looked like London on Sunday. After breakfast I crossed the Rivoli; and as I live by bread I could see only two cabs about a mile and a mile-and-a-half off respectively, and not twenty people beween me and the horizon. In the afternoon we went to the Place de la Republique, where Charlotte clung to lamp posts to see over peoples' heads, and got so furious when she saw a real crowd charged by real soldiers that she wanted to throw stones. By dignified strategy which did not at any time go to the length of absolutely running away, we left the field intact without wounds. In the evening we heard the Egmont overture, the choral fantasia (piano by Harold Bauer, who acted it capitally) and the 9th Symphony. The chorus piffled into the sky borders rather feebly; but a few pretty nuances were achieved by the sopranas—mostly, as usual, ladies in reduced circumstances. The four principals (from the Opera—this was at the Opera) were awful. When the basso rose to plead for more harmonious sounds after Beethoven's humorous and even attractive cacophony, this creature set up—in French —an obscene and staggering uproar such as I never heard in my life, nearly splitting on the F. sharp (I wish he had). The chorus stuck to Schiller's German and when the basso roared "Joie!" replied soberly "Freude" with rebukeful effect. So it went on, the operaorers singing "flemme prise au throne de Dieu" against the choral "Gotterfunken," and the soprano indignant and bewildered because Weingartner wouldnt stop the band to let her smile and take breath in the wrong place. None of the four had ever heard of Beethoven, or could conceive that the public cared more for the band and the conductor than for them; but the tenor, after some perplexed listening, rose to the occasion and was bully. Frantic demonstrations at the end.

Yesterday (Sunday) the elections, and the Canard Sauvage at the Théâtre Antoine. The garret scene was admirable; but there would not be room for it at the Court. It was played at great speed, and raced at the end of every act to get a curtain. Gregers, described by Relling as an expectorator of phrases, went full steam ahead all through. There was no character in Gina nor in old Ekdal—indeed there was no character in the acting at all as we understand it, but it was a bustling piece of work (to conceal Ibsen's deficiences, no doubt); and Relling brought down the house in the end when he rounded on the Expectorator. Hjalmar enjoyed himself enormously, and was amusing and convincing. Hedvig's voice was the voice of experienced and authorative maturity; but she pulled off her pathos with professional efficiency. Stage management ad lib: Gregers and his father walked ten miles in the first act if they walked a foot.—I must finish—Esmond be blowed!—(slipped and fell today in the Boul St. Germaine and tore my trousers scandalously in the face of all Paris)—We went to a Socialist election meeting on Saturday. It was just like any other Socialist meeting where the candidate has no chance and knows it.—Tomorrow I sit to Rodin for the last time; and we leave Paris for London by the 4 o'clock train.—All my photographs (9 dozen) are ruined by a defect in the shutter of my most expensive camera. Love to Lillah.

G.B.S.

When Captain Brassbound *finished,* You Never Can Tell *was revived on 9 July for "a limited number of weeks," with Lillah McCarthy as Gloria for the first time, and Henry Ainley as Valentine. Miss McCarthy's was an exquisite performance, to which Ainley's was by no means equal; after Barker he was uninspired. Shaw had written to Tita Brand when the matinees had finished the previous summer referring to Barker:*

My dear Tita,

You evidently *dont* like him, or you would not so completely overlook his share in your grievance. Egobetical and unreasonable young woman as you are, HOW could he tell you "straight out" that "your work did not suit him" when he was going to share your fate? Do you realise that after all his trouble and his very clever performance, he is now told that he is no use as Valentine—that he can draw teeth but not make love &c &c &c &c—all manner of unpleasant things. And all *your* fault, because you didnt care about Valentine and didnt pretend to.

The worst of it is that though we can perhaps substitute Ainley for Barker, I am by no means sure that we shall be able to get a really sympathetic Gloria for him who is at the same time strong enough to play the masterful side of the young lady; and in that case you will prance about worse than ever. I think I shall write a play for you about Boadicea. You are a walking thunderstorm.

Now, after more than a year, with a new cast for the play except for Norman Page, J. H. Barnes, Louis Calvert and Hazel Thompson, Shaw wrote to Miss Brand's mother:

She should come and see my nice new Gloria, who had the good sense to marry Tita's Valentine instead of prancing at him in public scorn and terrifying the Court audiences out of their wits.

Shaw, who had been abroad, went to a performance of the play on 14 July when he found "a degree of infamy which took away my breath." This was after Granville Barker's rehearsing.

Tentillie, Mevagissey, R.S.O. Cornwall
(until 5th. Sept.)
19th July 1906.

Address as above.

What was the name of the author of that play?

I went to see Y.N.C.T. on Saturday the 14th. The first half of the performance attained a degree of infamy which took away my breath. The first act was bad, but the second act was devilish—drily, industriously clever—every touch of grace and feeling forgotten—every point rushed and muffled—blasted, arid, cackling, tedious, forced—the thing moved like an unskilfully galvanized lay figure, not even like a corpse. I went round and expressed my opinion to Ben Webster at the stage door in the presence of Trevor Lowe.

Fortunately the play recovered itself in the 3rd. and 4th. acts, which were good. Barnes was exceptionally good all through: his 3rd act immense, as I had just told him that he had saved the performance and was the only entirely faultless actor now living. Page was all right except for the first 10 minutes, when the presence of his Prince deprived him of speech and motion. Dolly did not give a damn for anybody or anything and pegged away nobly all through.

Ainley is a vile dentist: he has a soul above it. After the way you wallowed in it, he cuts a poor figure when the forceps is in his hand.

We have ruined Gurney between us. Tell him that "She told you what I am—a father—a father robbed of his children" is all right as a frantic retort to Valentine, but that he must then collapse, and begin "What are the hearts of this generation" brooding brokenheartedly to himself. Also, the exit with his back to the audience was all very well for your pathetic version but it spoils the strong one—the nod is unintelligible.

G.B.S.

P.S. We can put you up here and give you a room to write in if

you like. The journey ended in a headache for me. Bathing
ad lib.

P.S. Calvert now forgets all the "oh *verys*" although they are the
surest laugh drawers in the part.

John Bull's Other Island *was to be cast for a six weeks' revival
starting on 17 September. Larry was to be played by Ben Webster
and Keegan by William Poel. The next letter contains an ad-
mission by Shaw that he once thought of playing the latter part!
Robert Loraine, who had been playing* Man and Superman *in
America, had been spending a holiday with the Shaws. Shaw had
him in mind for Charteris in* The Philanderer.

Pentillie, Mevagissey, R.S.O. Cornwall.

29th July 1906.

Dear Barker,

You want a lot more holiday: your casting organ is utterly
deranged.

Webster would be a very good Larry. He is extremely like my
Uncle Fred. He could also do Keegan—at a pinch. What is
more, he could do Dick Dudgeon.

Now that Ainley is snapped up elsewhere, we want a new
Ernster Liebhaher (Primo Amoroso) unless you are prepared to
give up everything else for acting, which would be bad economy.
Now Webster, who has a fine touch of sardonic humor, is much
nearer what we want than anyone else available and discovered.
If you engage him for John Bull you will have at your disposal
the following combinations of Larry and Keegan, 1 Webster-
Poel, 2 Barker-Webster, 3 Webster-Barker. No. 1 would set you
free altogether. No. 3 would save you the trouble of learning a
new part. No. 2 would save the situation if Poel proved impossible as Keegan and Webster as Larry.

Hallard does not come in anywhere. Webster comes in everywhere. I think you quite miss his fitness for Larry. We tried to
get him for it before, when he was in America. Hallard-Poel
would not do. Webster-Poel, with you in reserve, I am quite
prepared to try with some interest. And it is really more important

for you to write than to act, at all events until the play now in hand is off your mind.

Webster is even a possible Tanner, which Hallard is not.

Your exact value as Larry is about twopence. The value of a new play by you, after the Voysey Inheritance, is at least sevenpence. As there is not the faintest sign of anything now coming up in *my* garden, you may even put it at sevenpencehalfpenny.

Engage Webster and dismiss the matter from your mind. There is nothing better on the cards.

Loraine returns to London tomorrow (the 30th)—address, Green Room Club. He talks of coming to see us on the 4th; but then he doesnt know where we are as yet. If you see him you might sound him as to whether he could Philander at the Court on occasion next year.

Vedrenne's notion of Beveridge as Keegan was not altogether a bad shot. But Keegan must be incorporeal, and B. couldnt be that. I thought it over myself once.

Keep us informed of your whereabouts.

G.B.S.

The possibility of a deputy for Barker had been discussed, but Shaw's suggestion of William Poel for the position must have been intended to frighten Barker, for, though he owed much to Poel, the ideas of the two men as to what constituted satisfactory acting and production were far apart. The idea of moving to the Savoy Theatre was already in the air.

Pentillie, Mevagissey, R.S.O. Cornwall
5th August 1906.

To H.G.B.

The enclosed photograph became mine for threepence in Truro, where it irradiated the whole town from the most expensive row in the window of the smartest stationer. I cannot keep it any longer: it disturbs my dreams. You, a mere husband, can handle it with impunity.

If you get Webster and Poel and wont play yourself, then clearly Webster will play Larry (and perhaps Dick Dudgeon) and Poel will play Keegan. Boucicault would be a mere luxury, as you could not keep Webster eating his head off whilst B played Larry. Boucicault might play Keegan, Anderson, Undershaft, even Broadbent, and Lord knows what; but as things stand you dont need him if you can secure Ben.

Would Poel be any use as a deputy producer for you? A combination of Boucicault and Poel would be excellent; but as Heaven has put them asunder, let no man join them.

I hope this foolish Savoy business will fall through. You are fooling about your holiday and your play. The next thing you have to do is to finish the play and produce it; then publish it with Ann Leete and Voysey in a single volume, with a preface.

This place works me with the most frightful intensity: I write all day. At my age it does not matter: at yours it is the worst possible economy.

What is "the C. for an L.M.D"?

Loraine is on the road hither, motoring. You had better follow him up pretty soon.

G.B.S.

Now Shaw tells Barker that The Doctor's Dilemma *can be announced. Sir Artegall in the play was renamed Sir Ralph Bloomfield Bonnington, as the following letter begins to indicate, and the part was played by Eric Lewis. A number of players left the cast of* You Never Can Tell *while it was running, but Henrietta Watson was not one of them. The performances of* How He Lied to Her Husband *at the St. James's Theatre, mentioned in the first paragraph, had been given by the original Court Theatre cast in the spring. At this time the H. G. Wells attack upon the Fabian Society's Executive Committee was in progress.*

Pentillie, Mevagissey, R.S.O. Cornwall
21st August 1906.

Dear Barker,

I do not quite know what to charge for Bashville. The Barbara matinees brought me in about £33 a week. Taking this as the basis of the calculation, and generously sharing equally with Masefield and Maeterlinck (two inferior authors with much shorter *prose* plays), I arrive at a fee of £11. per week of two performances, or say £10:10:0. In consideration of Vedrenne's medical expenses, I am willing even to take £3:3:0 per matinee. How does this strike you? It works out at 6 guineas a week, just half what I asked Alexander for How He Lied at the St. James's. After all, what is money? Dross.

I think the triple bill as good as it is in the nature of such a thing to be. Webster will do for Cashel and Hearn for Catewayo: their old parts. Henrietta Watson was the original Lydia; but the part hadly calls for a special engagement if she is not in stock just then, though I should like her to get something out of her old and hitherto unrewarded exertions.

When you are sending out your press paragraphs announcing your autumn and winter campaigns, you may definitely announce a new play by me entitled The Doctor's Dilemma, in which Miss Lillah McCarthy and Mr. Granville Barker will be supported by a London company.

I send you a letter I have had (a second one) from Holmes Gore, as I think he would be just right for Cutler Walpole. Beveridge for Sir Patrick, Eric Lewis (or the like) for Sir Artegall, Clare Greet (with beard) for Emmy, and perhaps Daly for Blenkinsop is as far as I have got with the casting. Ridgeon remains an unsolved problem. Wyndham would do very well. I am slightly tempted to suggest Grossmith as a possible Sir Artegall. You will have a deathbed scene (to please Archer) which will, both in sublimity and blasphemy, surpass anything that ever gave Redford a nightmare. The spectacle of a hopeless blackguard dying a beautiful and imposing death, with his wife adoring him, and everyone else in the room knowing the truth about him, will satisfy my soul completely.

The first act is divided into two sets—is finished in draft. The theme is so futile that I have no doubt I could finish it in time for December if necessary.

Tell Webb I have had his letter. I should like to know from you what state of mind Wells is in about the Fabians before I answer it.

G.B.S.

P.S. Mrs. Drinkwater wants to play Mrs. Clandon when Henrietta Watson leaves. DONT tell me that Henrietta is going to.

69

The following four letters are concerned with The Doctor's Dilemma.

Pentillie, Mevagissey, R.S.O. Cornwall

28th August 1906.

Dear Barker,

All I can say is that though I have stopped three days out of my work on the play to write in a section on the Denshawai executions into the John Bull preface, I have already finished the second act, and know what the other three (!) will consist of: in fact they have already sprung into being and need only inking in. If I could get a clean run at them without a stroke of paralysis, and without prefaces and proofs and German and French translations to correct, and Hungarian, Bohemian and German piracy lawsuits to conduct, I could finish before the end of September. As it is, all I can say is that to begin on October 24 (I shall be in Birmingham orating on the 22nd) is not absolutely impossible.

Never mind the cast: I have had enough of casting: we can pick up a cast in a week provided we are sure of Lillah. The really pressing business will be her dresses. Tell her she will need a morning walking dress for Act 1, a dinner dress with cloak and wraps for Act II, a home dress for Act III (rather quiet), an extraordinarily beautiful and as-fanciful-as-she likes costume for Act IV (an unheard-of stage effect depending on this *colpo di bellezza*), and finally a handsome carriage afternoon dress for Act V. This means that there will not be much change out of £100 so let Vedrenne look to it.

The first act will be divided into two scenes, but the other acts will be fairly swift and rapid; so that the whole play will not be as long as Barbara and Bull. Scenes: two interiors, one at Ridgeons, the other at Dubedats (the artist-husband is named Louis Dubedat), covering four acts and a night scene—the terrace of the Star and Garter at Richmond, with a dinner table. Calvert can play the waiter, who only says "Yes, sir" once, and nothing else.

The death scene will be a masterpiece. You must play Dubedat. Ainley might play him, of course; but he would look too honest and the enjoyment of the part would set you up for life. Sir Artegall Osborne is now Sir Ralph Bloomfield-Bonner (familiarly, B.B.). He might be played by Lyall Swete.

Eadie sends me a letter of yours demanding an engagement. We might work him in; but all casting is premature for the moment. Ridgeon is a difficulty, Wyndham being out of the question.

I have forgotten the date of John Bull. If you are sending out program-circulars, send me one. We come up to town on the 4th. probably. Are you sure you have not a full length copy of John Bull somewhere? If so, send it to me. The cut copy is no use for the printer.

G.B.S.

Pentillie, Mevagissey, R.S.O. Cornwall
29th Aug. 1906.

There is one condition on which you could escape Dubedat without prejudicing the piece or the business, and that is getting Du Maurier to play him. Until I have written the death scene I cannot say whether the part will go beyond him; but so far, in the comic scenes, he would be perfect. So keep this in mind as a possibility. Webster could do Ridgeon, I think. Beveridge, Swete, Holmes Gore, Ben Webster, Du Maurier, Clare Greet and Lillah, with a good serio-comic man for Blenkinsop (who gets important in Act II) and a capable utility man for Schutzmacher; thats the cast so far.

G.B.S.

Castle Haven Rectory, Castle Townshend,
Co. Cork.
24th Sept. 1906.

Sei reihig, sei ruhig, mein Kind: we must do the best we can with what we have. I am making Walpole fit Hearn all right. I *dont* want a heavy man for Ridgeon: I want a clever, rather queer man. Gurney has the pathos of a poor mouth much more than Gwenn. I have written to Webster to say that if he makes up Larry like Courtenay Thorpe as the angel Gabriel, and plays him to suit, he will not convince the management that

71

he is capable of the new part. I shall modify Ridgeon a little in the revision, which is a slower job than the writing was. I wish you knew Wright: you would see the sort of thing I want at once.

We shall stay here until the 7th. probably.

G.B.S.

Castle Haven Rectory, Castle
Townshend, Co. Cork.
28th Sept. 1906.

I send you by this post to the Court sketches of the scenes for Act I and II. The background of II is not Richmond Hill but the Thames Valley. For Act I I want the scene set like the Peacy act of Voysey; the pier glass should be painted with flowers, like the glasses in this house; so that you cant see anything in it and dont have to whiten it. For the 3rd act we must have the full depth of the stage and the usual square set: a door on each side, the L up in the 3rd entrance. For the 4th I should like to have the entrance door in the flat, C, or a door marked Private anywhere L. It is a rotten play: the first set is proving very unmanageable: cutting makes it horribly dull. I leave here on the 7th.

G.B.S.

Sir Almroth Wright was the specialist on whom Shaw modelled his Sir Colenso Ridgeon: the part was played by Ben Webster. In the last letter we learn of Shaw's sketches for the settings; these were in colour, examples of Shaw's not very great skill in water-colours.

At last, on 20 November, with Man and Superman *running in the evening bill,* The Doctor's Dilemma *was put on for eight matinees. Called a tragedy, really a satire on the medical profession, this ambitious work had a great reception. Desmond MacCarthy thought it "not among the best plays", but like everyone he was fascinated. Said A. B. Walkley: "A thoroughly 'Shavian' play, this, stimulating and diverting for the most part, occasionally distressing, now and then bewildering. O philoso-*

pher! O humorist! you mutter with gratitude. And then you whisper, with a half sigh, O Pierrot! O Faun!"

Ellen Terry wrote to Shaw on 28 November: "Oh I was, I was. I was interested, amused, thrilled."

On 16 December the play came into the evening bill "for six weeks only," following Man and Superman.

Shaw's heart was set on doing The Philanderer *referred to in the following letter. It is clear that Barker was opposed to the play, sharing the Webbs' objection to it.*

Ayot St. Lawrence, Welwyn, Herts.
28th December 1906.

Barnes would be the man for Cuthbertson if we could get him back in time. Hearn is no use for comedy, except where the point lies in his not being comic. He could do Paramore, but though he might work up Cuthbertson as he worked up Ramsden, he would not be happy in it, and would do a bad first night. Gurney would be better than he as Cuthbertson. McComas can keep.

It is snowing; and I have to make my way to the Fabian Exec. and back again this evening.

If you want to produce, finish your own wretched play and produce it. Nothing would induce me to let you touch The Philanderer: you are longing to queer its pitch because you are ashamed of it. Well, I am proud of it. It is the best of my plays; and when I work it up with a little extra horse play it will go like mad. If I am disabled by any accident, Webster shall produce it (he'd do it very well: he has real humor and invention in this line) and you can play Charteris if you want to be in it somehow. And dont seduce Lillah into being unfaithful to me over it. By the way you must blight Vedrenne by telling him that Charteris is a costume part: the brown evening suit, blue shirt and sandals are clearly costume. There must be a good piano, a door that can be BANGED, a statue &c &c &c— about £100 worth of properties.

G.B.S.

73

A depressing financial statement for the year, caused Shaw to write to Vedrenne on 22 January 1907:

I am on the economical tack just now; that balance sheet is hard to swallow. The stars did not pay . . .

He was referring to Ellen Terry.

The Philanderer was then given seven matinees starting on 5 February. There was much heartburning; Shaw could not get the cast he wanted, and his friends did not like the play at all. Lillah McCarthy had rehearsed Julia, though "I loathed the play like hell" she said, to be in harmony with Barker, but she was carried off at the dress rehearsal to the Homoeopathic Hospital to be operated upon, and Mary Barton took over her part. Walkley called it "one of Mr. Shaw's least happy experiments", and without its leading player it did not please the audience, though today it is seen to be much above anything done by any of the popular dramatists of that day.

Shaw wrote to Vedrenne on 27 February a letter that should be inserted here. There had been much criticism of the length of Major Barbara, especially of the interminable final act. But Shaw would not listen:

I have revised Major Barbara. It will now play another ten minutes; but otherwise it will be its old self more than ever. You might as well dream of diluting the Atlantic Ocean as cutting Barbara down to an ordinary bill. You had better issue two-night tickets; one night for Acts I and II and the other for Act III: for the play in one piece is beyond human endurance. Further it will require at least a month's rehearsal, as Bill and Barbara will not be able to rehearse their scenes at home at all hours as the Yorkes did.

He went on to discuss the cast for a revival (which did not take place), and insists on having Barker as Cusins as in the original production the year before:

Cusins requires an actor of subtlety and refinement, with plenty of ingenuity and some comedy; or else it requires an actor with great beauty of voice and engaging personality . . . Barker has chucked Ainley because Ainley "will not play the game", which is like Barker's cheek, as he (Barker) plays the game much less than Ainley, giving the wretched author merely the leavings of his exhausted energy and preoccupied attention. Now let him get me another Ainley, or else play Cusins himself. If I am to be actor-managered out of all my decent leading men (not to mention the disgraceful disablement of Julia and consequent ruin of the Philanderer—in which Barker ought to have played Chateris) I shall go and be actor-managed by Alexander, who appreciates me more than ever now that my mother has a vote in South St. Pancras.

A second Ibsen play, Hedda Gabler, *was to be given seven matinees starting on 5 March with Mrs. Patrick Campbell in the leading part, and Shaw wrote to Barker as follows:*

10 Adelphi Terrace, W.C.
5th Feb. 1907.

I can't cast it. The only way to do it cheaply is to let Scott Brinst play his old part of Tesman, in which he can't be beaten; Nigel Playfair play Brack, for which he has just the figure, age and style; and you can play Lövborg.

Lövborg stands or falls by that first scene in which he asks Hedda how she could throw herself away on Tesman. If you can see L.I. doing that, I cant. It's a question of H.B.I. or Ainley, or you.

G.B.S.

Tesman	Brack	Lövborg
Scott Brinst	Charles Hawtrey	H. B. Irving
Hubert Harben	Allan Aynesworth	Henry Ainley
Sidney Brough	Holmes Gore	Lewis Casson
Kenneth Douglas	Laurence Irving	Martin Harvey
Dennis Eadie	De Lange	Hubert Carter
Cyril Maude	Nigel Playfair	Courtenay Thorpe
Cosmo Stuart	Sherbrooke	Basil Gill
Van Tempest	York Stephens	Granville Barker

Tesman	Brack	Lövborg
James Welch	Beerbohm Tree	
Louis Calvert	Harcourt Williams	
A. E. George	Bouchier	
Rudge Harding	Hubert Carter	
Lyall Swete	James Hearn	
Ben Greet	E. H. Kelly	
William Poel	Fred Kerr	
Trevor Lowe	Lablache (see description of Brack in text)	Understudies.
		Acton Bond
	Edmund Maurice	Rudolph de
	McKinnel	Cordova
	Kenyon Musgrove	Holthoir
	Norman Forbes	Dan McCarthy
	John Hare	Jules Shaw
	Sugden	

In fact, Trevor Lowe played Tesman, James Hearn Brack, and Laurence Irving Lövborg. After the dress rehearsal Shaw voiced his reactions:

10, Adelphi Terrace, W.C.
4th March 1907.

"Every blessed evening, with all the pleasure in life" is a vile line: it spoils the end of the play. Make him say "Regularly every evening: you may depend on me, Mrs. Tesman."

I wonder your hair is not grey; but it will be all right: you have got as much as there is to be got by management; and now you must let them rip in their own way. The last two acts will carry the day.

G.B.S.

The play was a success and Mrs. Pat was highly praised. She wanted it put on for a run, but Barker would not agree, and she quarrelled with him. In her letters she said that Barker attended the rehearsals and sometimes Shaw, but they left her alone.

The Silver Box *followed Shaw's play in the evening bill on 8 April, and on the following day there was a start with eight matinees of Elizabeth Robin's "dramatic tract"* Votes for Women! *This brilliant success did not please Shaw. He thought the casting wrong. Writing to Vedrenne he said, "Barker is altogether too clever a stage manager to be trusted in judging the relative importance of stage management and casting. He has come to think that it does not matter who acts as long as he produces". His conclusion upon the production of this play and that of* The Silver Box *was: "I therefore consider both productions disgraceful in the highest degree to the theatre". Shaw's criticism was for Barker's sake: the advice of a father to a son. When, on 29 April, St. John Hankin's* The Return of the Prodigal *appeared in the evening bill for "four weeks only" to prove an utter failure,* Votes for Women! *was substituted for it. Writing to Vedrenne Shaw shows how much he was aroused by what he considered to be bad management:*

I am greatly distressed by this Prodigal business, because it shows that neither of you understand what has made the Court possible. I have given you a series of first-rate music hall entertainments, thinly disguised as plays, but really offering the public a unique string of turns by comics and serio-comics of every popular type. Calvert as Broadbent and William, Gwenn as Straker, Lewis as B.B., Yorke as Bill, with the sisters Clandon and the Irish character turns and the newspaper man have done for the Court what George Robey and Harry Lauder have done for the halls. Make no error V.D. that is the jam that has carried the propaganda pill down. Even in Voysey it was the Booth turn, the Clarence turn, the wicked solicitor and the comic old woman that consoled the house for the super drama.

Why do you deliberately choose the worse play, the less popular play, the stale play, the play that didn't succeed? Barker doesn't see it; but then Barker has for months past been fit only for a padded room: a man who, with Cassilis under his hand could choose *Charity and the Reformer,* and with the *Campden Wonder* to produce could deliberately kill it by an impossible bill, is out of court. He wont write a play himself and wont produce any rival play except an obviously unworthy one. He wont act himself, and drives out of the theatre, on one pretext or another, everyone who could take his place. Until he gets a holiday and recovers his sanity the safe rule is to do exactly the opposite of everything he recommends. I have got that balance sheet badly on my mind; and it is becoming more and more apparent in the newspapers that now that the first scare is over, and something like the anti-boom has arrived, we must fight the press and whilst defying them by playing all the pieces they slate as if they were aces of trumps, take great care that the said pieces are highly entertaining as variety shows. With Lillah and Loraine we could make The Philanderer a humming success. Cassilis can be made the most amusing play in London. The *Campden Wonder,* in its proper place in a proper bill, can force the public to reverse the press verdict. Anyhow we must forget the press verdicts, as they are now becoming systematically hostile.

You can now get the other side from Barker and sum up yourself. I am not sure that The Silver Box ought not to have a turn. But as I have to send this note into town by my wife, who starts in two minutes, I must conclude, hoping you are well, as this leaves me at present, etc. etc.

The above is an important contribution to Shavian criticism, and shows Shaw disturbed by the failures, but the most serious was in fact Captain Brassbound's Conversion.

Prunella *had eight matinees starting on 7 May, and did very well.*

The document referred to in the following letter, which was intended to be read to "poor Vedrenne," is the second after this. Lady Lewis was the wife of Sir George Lewis. Shaw refers to a proposal that Barker should go to America to direct the New Theatre being built in New York and is considering who should carry on in his place. The play under discussion is Don Juan in Hell. *The costumes were to be designed by Charles Ricketts, and Shaw drafts a letter for Miss McCarthy, who was to play Ann, to send to Vedrenne. At this time the Wells' revolt in the Fabian Society was in full action, as the letter shows.*

Ayot St. Lawrence, Welwyn, Herts.

21st April 1907.

Dear Barker,

You are to take the enclosed to poor Tobit Vedrenne, and read it to him. When Lady Lewis asked me who else than you was available I could suggest nobody but Whelen. Whelen was in Germany at the time; and I have not yet said anything to him. I mention him to you because he is a man to bear in mind. He might be a possible locum tenens for you. Or he might be a rival for the sceptre of the American experiment and the English one that will come later. His present berth, next to yours, is the best jumping-off place in London.

It is blowing great guns here: I shudder to think of your crossing. However, it will be all over by the time this reaches you.

Did it strike you in Florence that the frescoes there solved the problem of the ideal proscenium and the sky border (to some

extent). Why not 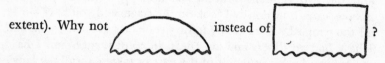 instead of ?

During your absence poor Lillah has been treated with the greatest brutality. She was—as far as I could guess—apprehensive and sentimental and a little weak in the spine. Two things are good when stiffening is wanted: strychnine and indignation. So I exploded on her the proposal about Irene Vanbrugh which Vedrenne (whose eyes are bad again) had exploded on me, and organized an epistolary bombardment of callous roughness and cruelty. The effect was excellent, Lillah supine and languorous before the letters, jumped up six feet high and lifted her chin to a very satisfactory angle. She has now forgiven the innocent Charlotte; and I shall presently blarney my way back into toleration; but for the moment, if domestic feeling runs at all against me, be careful not to defend me.

I reached the first Fabian Executive half an hour later, and found the new blood off the boil already—not even simmering. We have appointed the Committees; *and Wells has refused to be*

79

chairman of the Publishing Comtee. or even to serve on it at all!! You are on it. More when we meet.

Can you lunch at Adelphi on Wednesday—also Lillah if she is in town? Or could you run down here for a meal or a night or a moment in the meantime? No notice necessary, unless meat is desired.

Yr.
G.B.S.

P.S. Charlotte suggests that you come down by the 5.10 from Kings Cross on Tuesday; dine and sleep; and up next morning with me by the 8.58 train or with her by a later one (10.59)

My dear Mr. Vedrenne,

You are very unkind and obstinate about the dresses and I have a great mind to take away my husband and my author and shut up the Court Theatre. Only, as I could not take you as well, and the two gentlemen would be unhappy without you, and nobody cares how dowdy I look on the stage, and you have stolen all the sympathy from me by letting your eyes get bad again, and I have had an illness and am cheap in consequence, and I have spoiled you by my weakness in the past in taking a walking lady's salary from you, and I cannot force you to give me my £25. willingly and wont take it if you grudge it, and am not going to let you quarrel with me no matter how bad you try, and Mr. Shaw tells me that you are an angel and that I am only worth thirty shillings a week and find my own stockings and laces, I will indulge you just this once, and then go for ever to some theatre where they really appreciate hard work and good temper.

I shall buy my own dresses, and only ask you to put a line in the program—"Miss McCarthy's dresses have been supplied by Messrs. Brown & Wilkins, 789 Old Kent Road—23/11¾ the skirt and blouse—the hat a real bargain at six shillings."

I return the agreements, signed. After all, I am just as glad that the Superman one gives me control of my dresses. I hope you will like them.

And I really hope you are better, and that I have not worried you too much.

Barker—also Vedrenne

First, in reply to questions addressed to me by letter, which I tried to answer yesterday by telephone to Portman Mansions but could not, as they were repairing the line and had crossed the wires hopelessly:—

I have, as requested, sampled the program at the Court, and have to report as follows:

The Silver Box was all right except for Miss Hamilton, whose performance proved that Barker was capable of anything in the way of casting. In Votes For Women Miss Sterling McKinlay was also a very obvious miscast. She is quite impossible as an ingenue. She is a capable female like Miss Barton, and might be useful in certain parts; but—! ! ! ! ! ! ! ! ! ! ! ! I was much entertained by Aubrey Smith in the last act. He said, in effect, "At this point I have been requested by Mr. Granville Barker to do a waltz. Why, I dont know; but as he pays me for it, I have no objection. So here goes. One—two—three &c."

The moral is that Barker is altogether too clever a stage manager to be trusted in judging the relative importance of stage management and casting. He has come to think that it does not matter who acts as long as he produces. This is a deadly mistake. Get your cast right, and get them interested in themselves and in the occasion, and stage management can be done without, though it does no harm when it does not get into the way of the acting. Get your cast wrong; and you wreck your play just to the extent to which the cast is wrong. If Sydney Fairbrother and Dorothy Minto had played the loose lady and the ingenue respectively, and had come on at the wrong sides, fallen over the furniture, and finally pitched over the float into Stier's lap, their parts would still have lived and produced their effects. As it was, the stage business was as perfect as a quadrille: but the parts simply did not exist; and the plays were consequently produced with too large gaping holes in them. I therefore consider both productions disgraceful in the highest degree to the theatre. Let Barker go home and write plays. He has no real genius for stage management; only an arrant laziness which makes him busy himself on cheap detail when he ought to be doing something important and difficult.

Now as to the cast of the forthcoming performances. For a Season production we had better stick to Sarah Brooke: we want all the style we can cram on; and Sarah has style. Neither Hearn nor Barnes will do for the statue. Failing Hare or Lewis or some other mercurial high comedian, I will venture with Trevor Lowe. What is wanted is elasticity and gaiety, with social distinction—exactly what is sure to be engaged elsewhere doing fashionable plays, or musical comedy. If Lewis is inexorable I will coach Trevor. Sherbrooke would be better for the devil than McKinnel, who is too solid and heavy and locally English. The foreign touch in Sherbrooke is exactly what is wanted. Still, Mac's Pan was uncommonly good.

But I have just forgotten a frightful difficulty. If the Man of Destiny comes off, it will hardly be possible for Lowe to study two parts at once. It is true that the statue has not much to say; but still, the lieutenant has a good lot. I am half tempted to suggest Calvert as a possible lieutenant; but the two rival producers in the same play—Dot & Lewis—would be disastrous. McKinnel could do the lieutenant, of course; and there is always Goodhart.

Confound this casting! if I go on about it I shall be unable to deal with the serious part of this letter. Let me know when the rehearsals are to begin. I shall be down here at Ayot St. Lawrence until Wednesday morning.

Now as to America. There is a tide in the affairs of men, as our national bard has well observed. I am not sure that its flood may not be marked in your case by this proposal of Lady Lewis. The game is up at the Court: it has not yet begun at the Savoy. Four years is enough to give to any one move in the way of high art; witness my avatars as literary critic, musical critic, dramatic critic, &c. &c. Debating societies, which always begin on a wave of public interest in something, begin to die after four years; and the Court is nothing but a debating society. The Shaw boom, in its novelty phase, cannot last longer.

We have been chewing the cud of it for a year past; AND YOU CAME OUT TWO THOUSAND POUNDS TO THE BAD, but with a reputation and a management worth twopence in

London, but worth a million dollars to this American Committee. Why not do four years there, and then come back and found the national theatre and opera house of this country? You have the pick of the Court repertory to begin with, including Major Barbara and The Doctor's Dilemma, also Voysey and Prunella. You can make Stier's fortune, and give him eight horns and three trombones, with tubas and percussion ad lib. Barker can barkerize all my plays out of recognition without interference from me. You can trade off the Savoy to Robertson for Caesar, or to somebody else who wants a theatre. You can even relet it to Mrs. Carte at a profit when she repents, or to someone who believes that there is life yet in Gilbert and Sullivan.

Think it over. But remember that Spenlow and Jorkins are inseparable. And I think the idea of attaching Stier is an important one. Failing Nikisch or Mottl or Siegfried Wagner, he is as good as you will get, and much better than most and he will work with you in a way that no stranger would.

Eventually, simultaneous operations on both sides of the Atlantic might be possible. Finally you will be shoved out in the course of nature by the men you will train and clear the way for; but in the meantime, AS THAT PROCESS STARTS FROM THE VERY BEGINNING AND IS ALREADY IN OPERATION you must move up at every opportunity.

This, in view of the possibility of the project coming to nothing, is enough for the present.

Yours ever
G.B.S.

The above important letter was intended to be a highly serious communication to the joint managers on a number of subjects. It contains a rebuke to Barker (also to Vedrenne) for wrong casting of The Silver Box. *The casting of* Don Juan in Hell *and* The Man of Destiny *is dealt with, and Shaw urges Barker to take the American proposal seriously. He thinks the Shaw novelty is over, which did not mean more than is suggested by the word "novelty", and he wants Barker to consider what America might do for his career. Stier, conductor of the orchestra at the Court, was a very capable musician. Barker's uncertain mind is made evident by what Shaw writes. Fernhurst, near Hindhead, referred to at the opening of the following letter, is where the Barkers had a cottage.*

Shaw was rehearsing Robert Loraine as Tanner in Man and Superman. *The actor had produced the play in New York as long before as 5 September 1905. In his biography his wife says of the rehearsals for the American production, "He tried out and dismissed thirteen Strakers, four Tavy's, history does not record how many Ann Whitefields, or . . . Papa Hector Malones." The revival at the Court was to start on 21 May with Loraine playing under Shaw's direction, not his own. Shaw had great hopes of Loraine when he knocked him into shape, and even considered him as a successor to Barker.* Don Juan in Hell *is also discussed, as well as* The Man of Destiny *to be played with it.* John Bull's Other Island *and* You Never Can Tell *were to be sent out on tour with Louis Calvert.*

10, Adelphi Terrace, London, W.C.
May 24th 1907.

Dear Barker,

I am in two minds about going down to Fernhurst on Sunday. If I have to rehearse Destiny on Monday morning, which seems possible, I should hardly be able to get up in time. I am also faintly curious to see a Pioneer performance on Sunday evening. Ordinarily I should not think of staying in town for it; but Charlotte has gone off in a motor car to hunt for a house in the river district; and the result is that I find myself going in for all manner of games which I never dream of when I am a married man. For instance, I have only been two nights by myself; and the first night I went to the Adelphi to hear Offenbach's Contes d'Hoffman, which was quite worth hearing; and yesterday, my vicious habits growing on me, I actually went to the Empire to see Genée dance.* I have not seen Vedrenne for some time; but before I despatch this letter I will try to get on to Mrs. Phyllis through the telephone and find out how he is.

In the theatre, the state of things would break your heart. I have destroyed the very last remnants of discipline. Loraine, who

* Last night, Joan of Arc, Sothern-Marlowe.

always starts a Company by sacking at least three members of it after the first rehearsal to intimidate the rest, is aghast, and has impulses, which recur at intervals of ten minutes, to take the next boat back to America and leave you to play Tanner. I have assimilated all of his business that is to the good so instantaneously that he is quite unconscious of any of it having been assimilated at all, whilst I have so utterly rejected the starry part of it that he is in consternation and despair. The motor car is now—I was going to say in the middle of the stage, but as a matter of fact it is all over the stage, like your dining table in Voysey. He wanted to deliver the great speech about the tyranny of mothers enthroned in the motor car, with Lillah somewhere under the wheels with her back to the audience. I immediately saw the value of the idea, and put Lillah in the car in a fascinating attitude with her breast on the driving wheel, and Loraine ranting about on the gravel. He declares that this is the utter ruin and that I might as well put on your understudy at once; but his dismay imparts an invaluable quality of earnestness to his acting. He feels that he is on the brink of a catastrophe, which is exactly what one wants from Tanner. He acts extremely well in the style of Wyndham. His vigour is apparently inexhaustible: even when he tires he presently gets a perfect tornado of second wind and goes stronger than ever. He has got all the comedy side of the part capitally, and does it quite in my old-fashioned way, with a relish and not under protest, like you. He keeps the play very tense and bright and lively whilst he is at work; but he has evidently had to carry the whole play on his own shoulders in America; and he has played it from beginning to end as comedy. He has quite missed the peculiar intimacy of the Robinson-Whitefield family circle; he has left the poetry out altogether; and he has never given Tanner away to Ann: in fact, it is pretty plain to me that he has never had an Ann to give himself away to. You can imagine that with all this readjusted for him after 500 nights of playing it the other way, he is pretty miserable. He looks gloomier and gloomier every day; but he keeps his temper admirably—not perhaps like an angel, but at all events like a very capable demon. I am hoping that he will begin to feel the new business before Monday night: if not, perhaps he will feel it when he has an audience to bite on it. Meanwhile Don Juan has been absolutely suspended, as Loraine is so disoriented that he wants three times as many rehearsals of the Superman as there is time for; and as I cannot let him rehearse the Hell scene on Monday (it is frightfully exhausting) we shall only have from Tuesday to Tuesday to get Hell into order. To add to the confusion McKinnel is stage managing the Pioneer performance for Sunday next; and he seems to have got the whole Court Company into it. Altogether I shall have everybody's nerves in a highly sensitive state for the first night. Whatever else there will be there will not be any staleness.

I enclose you the manuscript of an analytical programme for Don Juan. I think we ought to print it either on the programme or on a spare leaf to be distributed with the programme. There is no use in leaving the wretched critics to discredit the whole affair by their misunderstandings. Hitherto the first thing we have always had to do with a new play is to live down their confounded follies. In future we had better tell them what to say and what to think beforehand. It will save some of the mischief, if not all of it.

I have written to Calvert to 53a Shaftesbury Avenue. His reply is not yet to hand. I have urged on him that he must let No. 1 towns see the new Calvert of Broadbent and Bohun or else he will be trading on an out-of-date reputation.

Our minds seem to have jumped together as to McKinnel. I should not now hesitate to try him as Undershaft: in fact, I have now ticked down Barbara as a possible early revival. I found I was right about the Hell scene; both McKinnel and Sherbrooke are fitted perfectly, and would be ghastly if they exchanged parts.

When Vedrenne is well enough to bear it I want to cross him on one point. The more I think of it the more I am convinced the we must not put up The Devil's Disciple or any other play, except perhaps You Never Can Tell, for eight weeks; and I only except You Never Can Tell because it has been revived so often that no revival is now likely to be mistaken for a run. Six weeks is the limit for The Devil's Disciple; and I would almost make a stand for four weeks at first productions if it were not that it means such a devil of a lot of rehearsing and producing.

If anything comes of the American project, Loraine is a youth to be very carefully considered. He is far and away the best alternative to yourself that we have been able to find. Just at present he loathes the Court. The shabbiness of the motor car and of Ramsden's study, the absence of his beautiful trees laden with chestnuts and the grassy banks round which he used to drive the motor, above all, what he calls the amateur acting, and my deliberate smudging out of the trade finish and disciplined smartness which is a point of honour with him, are all straining his devotion to myself to the very utmost. But when he gets into touch with the Court audience and begins to understand the game a little, his sufferings will be mitigated. With Lillah, he would make the Philanderer a tremendous success; and indeed I think that if you take the linch-pin out of our London applecart by going to New York, he could keep it going better than anybody else now in sight. However, we shall see what will happen on Monday night. I hope he will have quite a considerable success, because he is going through a fearful trial, and if he does not succeed he will blame me for it, and lose faith in Der Meister.

Lillah appears to be completely re-established. When she saw what Loraine wanted in the second act, she promptly came down the stage and turned her back to the footlights like a schoolgirl; and poor Loraine was publicly informed that it was all right, as she had been many years with Wilson Barrett and quite understood. This was additionally hard on Robert, as, to do him justice, he really believed he had been doing the best for everybody, and perhaps had been if they were rather a poor lot.

Beveridge turned up today, looking extraordinarily youthful, and apparently with all the crustiness mellowed out of him with American success.

G.B.S.

Granville Barker, Esq.,
Vann Cottage,
Fernhurst.
P.S. I had just settled the Destiny rehearsal for the afternoon and decided to come down to Haslemere by the 5 train tomorrow evening when Charlotte blasted me with a telegram to say she

would end her tour at Ayot on Saturday (tomorrow) afternoon. As she telegraphed on the wing I cannot get at her to stop her. I have fired off two telegrams to off-chance addresses, reply paid; but no reply has come: and it is close on post hour. If I can establish communication I will come, and let you know by wire.

Calvert refuses: his contract with Harrison seems conclusive. This means that I must decide about Broadbent; but I cannot make up my mind.

I have just talked to Vedrenne through the telephone: he has had a relapse as to his eyes and is suffering as before from pain and want of sleep; but his chest is still vibrating reassuringly. He proposes Graham Browne for Larry and Valentine, and, as G.B. is available and wants the engagement (for 6 months) I think this is much the best proposal so far.

G.B.S.

While Man and Superman *was running in the regular bill, the last of the matinee performances opened on 4 June with a programme consisting of* Don Juan in Hell *and* The Man of Destiny. *A proposal to do the Don Juan scene from* Man and Superman *had been made by Florence Farr in December 1905, she playing Ann; Shaw was not averse to it, but emphasized the difficulties, and suggested that Barker might lend the Court—which of course he would never have done—but nothing came of it.* Don Juan *had costumes designed by Charles Ricketts, as Shaw intended, and was played by Robert Loraine, Lillah McCarthy, Michael Sherbrooke, and Norman McKinnel. The result was one of the finest of all the productions at the theatre, and the acting was superb. Writing some time later about this production to Lillah McCarthy, Charles Ricketts said:*

"Of Shaw as a producer you are able to say more than I am. I was delighted with his method of training by lucid pieces of acting and explanations of difficult passages; and he avoided interruptions and noisy exclamations so usual at rehearsals; in this respect he is nearer the French standard, where speech is even over studied; in England too much attention is given to business. I will confess, however, that I thought the two hours dialogue

before a blank curtain a possible strain on the audience and suggested that, at a signal given by Mephistopheles, four guilded thrones should rise from the floor, to the strains of Mozart's minuet in Don Giovanni, a lit chandelier descend from the roof, and the black curtains part before an altar bearing flowers and candles surrounding a gilded Venus de Medici. Shaw, I think, rather approved, or said he did, but Barker told us we had neither the trap doors nor space nor the funds for this. Do you remember you rehearsed in a canvas cage to get used to your Velasquez period hoop, while the huge decorated helmet I modelled for Sherbrooke hurt his head. I still owe Shaw a grudge that he would not face the difficulty of persuading Loraine to forego a costly garment of purple velvet studied with rubies, he had brought from America, for the dress I had designed. Let me add, there was no trouble, Loraine was charming."

After the close of the season on 29 June 1907 a complimentary dinner was given to the two managers at the Criterion Restaurant on 7 July with the Earl of Lytton in the chair. There were two menus, one being vegetarian, for Barker at that time was a vegetarian as well as Shaw. H. Beerbohm Tree proposed the toast of the "Authors of the Court Theatre," in a long and characteristic speech not wholly devoted to the subject. In Shaw's equally lengthy, wittier and more strictly appropriate reply, he referred to the other Court playwrights, saying of Barker's playwriting that its "delicacy and sublety requires exquisite handling," and that "It is Vedrenne's just boast that he has produced Barker," and commending Gilbert Murray, Masefield and St. John Hankin's work. The speech was noteworthy for its attack upon the press:

"The difficulties of the enterprise have been labours of love, except in one unfortunately very trying respect. There has been no sort of satisfaction in the unremitting struggle with the London press, which from first to last has done what in it lay to crush the enterprise. I know this uncompromising statement will surprise some of you because in any newspaper you see praises of Vedrenne and Barker, ecstasies over the Court Theatre acting, paragraphs about the most frequently played Court author and so forth.

That has become the fashion and the indiscriminate way in which it is done shows that it is done as a matter of fashion rather than of real appreciation. But if you turn back from this new convention to the points at which newspaper notices really help or hinder management—to the first night notices of the first productions—you will see what I mean. There you will find a chronicle of failure, a sulky protest against this new and troublesome sort of entertainment that calls for knowledge and thought instead of the usual cliches."

This violent and by no means unjustifiable attack concluded with the sentence:

". . . a damp cloud of grudging, petulant, ill-conditioned disparagement, suggesting to them that what they had been working so hard at was not a play at all, but a rather ridiculous experiment which was no credit to anybody connected with it."

At the close of Shaw's speech the management of the restaurant interposed with the information that as the time had passed eleven o'clock the proceedings must end, so the expected speeches by Professor Gilbert Murray, Miss Edith Wynne-Matthison, Sir Oliver Lodge and William Archer were not delivered. These speeches, were, however, included in a printed report.

Writing to Charles Ricketts the day after the affair Bernard Shaw referred to the last production at the Court Theatre:

When I arose to speak last night it was five minutes past eleven and the Commendatore from Scotland Yard was knocking at the door, consequently I had to give up all idea of saying anything of importance. I should, however, have liked very much to have brought out the artistic significance of our Don Juan experiment. It seems to me that we (I say "we" much as an organ-blower uses the plural pronoun when speaking of the organist's performance of a Bach fugue) hit on a most valuable and fascinating stage convention. William Morris used always to say that plays should be performed by four people in conventional costumes, the villain in a red cloak, the father in a bob-wig, etc. etc. etc., and I have always loved Harlequin, Columbine, Sganarelle, etc. in eighteenth century Italian Comedy and French Champetre painting. If only we could get a few plays with invisible backgrounds and lovely costumes like that in a suitable theatre, with fairy lights all round the proscenium, there would be no end to the delight of the thing . . .

P.S. Shall we do a pantomime for Christmas at the Savoy—a real pantomime?

Ricketts replied:
. . . the interruption of the police I viewed as a ruse (by the alleged Vedrenne) to stop possible lectures by learned professors . . .

Arrangements for the Savoy Theatre season were well in hand before the Court season ended. Shaw had written to J. E. Vedrenne on 3 May 1907 objecting to a proposal to form Vedrenne-Barker into a limited company:

. . . all that you would gain by the change would be the rather questionable alteration of Vedrenne and Barker to Vedrenne and Barker Limited, and a call on me in the event of a smash, the possibility of which would compel me to give much more of my mind to the management than I can spare for my other work. It would also lead to the most fearful rows with Barker . . .

An important letter was addressed by Shaw to Vedrenne on 27 July:

£2000 is all I can guarantee. I have barely £3000 loose at the bank; and I cannot get on with less than £1000 under my hand to produce the necessary effect of being a millionaire. It is not so easy to draw up the conditions. What I propose as a basis for discussion is that we lodge £4000 to a separate account as a guarantee fund, I contributing £2000 and you and G.B. £1000 apiece. This will be a real proceeding on my part and a purely paper one on yours.

Interest on this sum at the rate of 5% is to be a first charge on V. & B.'s business, payable monthly or quarterly. This will be also a real proceeding as regards me and a paper one as regards you. Its effect will be that you will have an interest in getting rid of the fund as soon as possible. Considering the risk, I ought to have 30% at least; but as a Socialist and a Man of Feeling, I am willing to make you a present of 25%.

The paying off of my £2000 is to be a final charge on the profits of V. & B. (total profits for London and the provinces), profits to be reckoned after salaries of £1000 a year apiece to V. & B. have been charged as expenses. Barker also, of course, to draw salary and fees as author and actor at the rate of £5. per act, and fees on not more than the Shavian scale. My own salary—another thousand—is to be taken out in moral superiority.

The guarantee fund shall not be drawn upon for current expenses at the Savoy—but it shall be available in the last resort to secure the rent payable by you as lessee of the Savoy for the season ending Easter 1908.

On 1 August Shaw wrote again to insist:

I am not going into partnership: I shall simply act as a usurer.

and later in the month, writing from Heidleberg, on the 19th, in a letter addressed to Messers. Vedrenne and Barker he says:

I reluctantly enclose £350. £100 of it, I am told, for Superman scenery.

The last sentence refers to a tour of the play. Shaw was concerned to keep everyone up to the scratch for the new venture at the Savoy, and it seems clear that he was bothered about its prospects. Writing to Vedrenne on 16 August he says:

Barker actually talks of Congreve and Shakespeare because he finds everything else barred by his reluctance to tackle anything but easy plays and easy people—easy, that is, to his temperament. And what are you to do if he goes to America . . . ?
Barker wont have anybody but Lillah, and you wont have Lillah . . . I can let you have the guarantee money as soon as you like.

A letter to Barker about an actor, Hubert Carter, is noteworthy for its criticism of Barker himself. Carter first appeared on the stage in 1889, and had played with Forbes-Robertson and others, did Macbeth for William Poel, and appeared in Gordon Craig's productions of Ibsen's The Vikings *and* Much Ado About

Nothing. *He played Jason in* Medea *at the Savoy, playing the same part later with Sybil Thorndike.*

10 Adelphi Terrace, W.C.
15th June 1907.

I send you the enclosed, not knowing what else to do with it. Carter is a quite hopeless creature who would have to be taken by the scuff of his neck and forced into a part without the least regard for his feeling or his enormous reflectiveness and discursiveness; but he has a most remarkable mug and could do certain character parts well. Besides, he can be useful to anybody except himself. On the whole, put him on your list. He has a chronic depression and delicacy that should make him a man after your own heart for your own plays. Bumptiousness for me!

G.B.S.

There was trouble at the Savoy before the season started. Vedrenne was ill, and occupied with other theatrical business. It appears that he was already prepared to close down in the spring of the following year, which in fact was what happened. He seems to have been ready to consider Peer Gynt, *which Shaw was so persistently trying to get Barker to do. Gilbert Murray's version of* Medea *appeared later on at the Savoy, but Miss McCarthy did not play in it.*

10 Adelphi Terrace, W.C.
22nd June 1907.

I heard such anguish of mind in V's voice through the telephone yesterday morning that I went to Portman Mansions and talked to him. He said you declared you could not rehearse four plays simultaneously and that I must come back from Wales in September to help. I heroically consented; but if you covet the lot, you are welcome to it. The D's D. is just the sort of play you like to amuse yourself with; and I havent the heart to meddle with you; so do your worst. The Hamilton geneille (girl) will do very well for Essie, accent and all. Why on earth do you want to supplant her now that there is a little chance for her? Your treachery to your wretched subordinates is revolting.

V.D. wants to shut up at Easter and hand the shop over to Mrs. D'O.C. for the summer season, finishing with Peer Gynt. By the way, you had better let *me* produce P.G. and play Peer yourself in the first two acts. The old Peer should be played by a real old man. A complete performance would have you for the young Peer, Eric Lewis for the Sphinx-Anitra episode and Farren for the finale.

Loraine wants to go to America for money and come back as he did this year for art. But this will not fit in with the D'O.C. scheme. As to Medea, Lillah will not be a bit of use for that: I want her for certain of my plays exclusively, with intervals of lucrative adventures. If you are serious about Medea, we must get Janet a new set of teeth; she is the only woman who can touch it. Lillah, by the way, would be enormous as Hecuba, she would be a most beautiful and weird old woman. Her Medea would have holes in it, and that wont do. Not that I do not appreciate the sound experience of Mrs. Crummles (Charrington also had his phase of admiring "that woman, Sir"); but holes is holes and Medea is Medea. Here endeth the statutory limit in portents.

G.B.S.

There are two letters to Vedrenne about the tour of John Bull's Other Island *at this date in which Nigel Playfair was to play Broadbent.*

10th June 1907.

Playfair is not a useful safe man; but he is a leading man; and that is what we must have.

20 July 1907.

Playfair is a treasure to us. If he could do as well as he did without a single rehearsal at Margate what will he be after a weeks drill at the Savoy? If need be I will come up and take him in hand. I know exactly what he needs: it is all as easy as A B C. You will never get your eyes well if you let Barker load up his worries on to you. Keep your eyes on your author, and he will pull you through.

Rosina Filippi referred to in the following letter first appeared on the stage in 1883 and played Catherine in Arms and The Man *when it was done at the Savoy. She ran a notable school for the stage which Shaw had just visited, before going for a holiday.*

10, Adelphia Terrace, W.C.
5th July 1907.

I walked into Rosina's parlor today to see a rehearsal of Candida by her pupils. The Eugene was quite a possible successor to you in the part—a youth to be snapped up promptly. Will you make an appointment with him and see what you think of his appearance. I have said nothing to him to suggest that I thought anything particular of him; but all he wants is some practice in a big theatre to be a very high class juvenile indeed. If he had any comedy in him he would make a very elegant Phil; but as far as I could guess, he joks wi deefficulty. Anyhow, see him. Address Leslie Hamer, Arundel Chambers, Arundel Place, Haymarket. The Lexy was also heavenborn—one Ashton K. Pearce.

G.B.S.

The Shaws were at a Fabian Summer School. The play referred to below was John Bull's Other Island, *which Barker had rehearsed for the tour. Nigel Playfair (already mentioned) started his stage career as an amateur and first appeared as a professional in 1902 at the age of twenty-eight; he played Hodson in the original production of Shaw's play. He was, as Shaw says, a born actor, and a personality on the stage. He afterwards became a distinguished manager. William Poel's enterprise of which Shaw complains was a production of* The Merchant of Venice *at the Fulham Theatre. The letter is fatherly advice to the head-strong moody Barker. Mrs. Cholmondely was Mrs. Shaw's sister.*

Hafody Bryn, Llanbedr, Merionetheshire, R.S.O.
20th July 1907.

My dear G.B.

Why kill yourself with unnecessary anxieties? There is absolutely nothing to worry about. You *would* have your scratch performance and you *would* worry because it was not like Voysey after three weeks drilling at the Court. I didn't want the scratch performance, because I knew what it would be like. Nigel fulfilled my expectations to a hair's breadth. I calculated him rightly for Margate; and I believe I am calculating him right for Manchester. He is a perfect godsend. If you cant cure him, with one word, of making Broadbent a CAD, I can; but neither you nor I can cure Louis of making him a hippopotamus and revolting people who cannot melt over a baby of that species. Nigel needs about three hours coaching to make him all right. First, he is to dress like a gentleman for the first act; and change back to it during the Larry-Nora scene in Act IV. He has to be taught the proper platform intonations for the political windbaggery; to be taken carefully through the phosphorus frills scene; to be shewn two or three touches in the second love scene (the first is all right—"will you be my wife" is a rude point of mechanism) and there you are! Of course it will not be Calvert; but then in the nature of things the future history of J.B.'s O.I. must be a history of broadly comic Broadbents, and not happy accidents like Calvert's personality. It is far better that the provinces should get the part from Playfair, who can give it to them again, or be reproduced by a successor, than in the irreproducible way. I repeat, again and again, if you cant handle Playfair, you cant manage a theatre: you can only do what the others do—train worms to play your own game. No doubt it is a very good game; but it is not *the* game. Playfair is a born actor, just as Gurney is. You hate the thing because it is so blatant and unreal—because it is a garish projection of an overemphasized personality; but it draws and pays. And my plays are built to stand that sort of thing. The provinces stand it and like it. You must make up your mind to supply it to the provinces, and to get back by it a good deal of money you will lose—or not make—at the Savoy.

Poor Vedrenne! How utterly barbarous of you to upset him for nothing, and force me to smite him in the waistcoat with a rattling bladder! I ask you, Granville Barker, what did you expect when you went to Margate? The Comedie Francaise, no doubt.

A detail. The grasshopper scene will not do in the provinces with that silly singer beer bottle. We must go to Tisley & Spiller or some other maker of laboratory apparatus, and get one of the little whistles with which they test how shrill a note you can hear. Tiny brass things, with pneumatic blowers attached. We ought to have used one all through at the Court, but I did not think of the device until too late.

Ricketts and I want to do a old Italian comedy of arts, with Watteau harlequinade—Sganarello, Dothore, etc. all complete (time—2007-8) for the Savoy. The costumes and curtains will cost about £2000.

If you dont want to kill yourself, dont try to do everything at the Savoy six times over. Make your casts as well as you can; and stick to them. You will not be any better able to choose on the 10th August than you were on the 10th July. Just think of all the time and worry and money you have wasted over John Bull for nothing.

I have just had to pay £15 to make up the deficit on Poel's week at the Fulham—loss £115. As I guaranteed something quite different, I have given the bankrupt enterprise a bit of my mind about it.

Mrs. Cholmondely has just arrived.

Let me know when and where you move.

G.B.S.

The Devil's Disciple was being cast for the Savoy season. The Shaws were on holiday and Shaw was clearing up his affairs after his labours in connection with the Court Theatre. He warns Barker against thinking of producing Congreve, a warning Barker respected; but Shakespeare was another matter.

Hafody Bryn, Llanbedr, Merionethshire, R.S.O.
3rd August 1907.

Million millions! We settled the Disciple cast ten times over. You would not have my Essies at any price, you had your own entire and perfect fit for it. We agreed on a string of 50 Swindons. Ingleton, Kenyon Musgrove (is that his name?), anybody not too soft and human in the Scotch way or sufficiently blusterous and Booth-Voysey like in the British way.

I am not dreaming of a play. I am revising translations, revising my will (now obsolete), drafting agreements with translators all over Europe, desperately trying to get my affairs into order after years of neglect at the Court, wrenching myself free from a perfect briar wood of unsettled affairs and loose ends and dead wires that ought to be electrified; so that if I die there may be some chance of Charlotte being able to make out how my copyrights &c stand.

The day you touch Congreve or Shakespear, Vedrenne and Barker die.

This is a beauteous place; but the weather is hideous. It rains inconceivably, and the air is so damp that it is a mere form to put a roof on a house. And one's spirits go up and down with the barometer.

G.B.S.

Hafody Bry. Llanbedr, Merionethshire,
10th August 1907.   R.S.O.

Casson is quite wrong for the lawyer, who must be a cool, smooth civil hand. He is all right for Brudenel and Detlive, the man who played the lawyer in Manchester, was all right for it. Singleton would be all right for it. I havnt written to V.D. about Poulton (mere procrastination); but he is certainly by chalks the best man for the part if he is bearable in his lay capacity.

Loraine has just arrived with a huge F.I.A.T. car, commissioned, it appears by Charlotte: and we—Ch. L. Mrs. Cholmondely and self are off to Snowden in it. I had rather stay here and work; but I suppose the airing (I have no motoring coat) is good for me.

The Fabian School is sleeping five in a room, and apparently enjoying it. Webb has been here in frightful weather. Charrington has promised. Janet has been offered by Flanigan (Manchester) the part of Queen Elizabeth in a heroic play by Calmour! She asks shall she take it or try for Medea. I have said take it.

G.B.S.

We see from the following letter that Barker is to produce The Devil's Disciple, *Shaw being still in Wales. Forbes-Robertson had*

played Dick Dudgeon in 1900. Vedrenne had to make up his mind
that Barker was to play General Burgoyne. Shaw had nearly
been drowned, the story is told in Loraine's biography by his wife.

Hafody Bryn, Merionethshire, R.S.O.
12th August 1907.

Dear Barker,

I knew you wouldnt be able to stage-manage D's D. The
business is all in the book: it worked so perfectly at the first
rehearsal that Robertson said "Oh, this is an easy play". The
doors are like this.

I have purposely put the fireplace on the same side in Acts

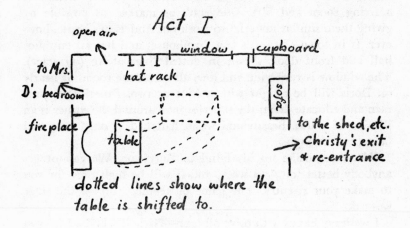

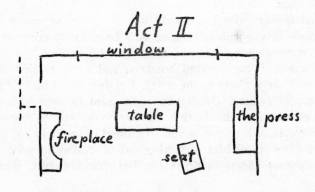

99

Act III

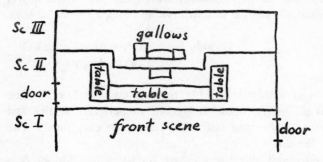

I and II, so as to make the contrast between Judith's notion of a living room and Mrs. Dudgeon's as marked as possible by giving them similar material to work on. Anderson's house, however, is in town (Mrs. D's is a farmhouse) and has an entrance hall and front door, shewn in dotted lines above (off stage). The window is very wide and low, all across the room, or nearly so. Doris will be alright with a hint or two. *Do* stick to your men and educate them: the superior man around the corner is an illusion of youth. Brassbound wasnt half bad, if only there had been room enough.

V.D. must make up his mind to Burgoyne. We cannot get anybody better for £5 a week, and it will be high time for you to make your re-entry. The game of keeping you off the stage wont do.

I wash my hands with olive oil soap—Nicholl's, and advise you to do the same.

The Savoy enterprise had a very narrow escape of losing its chief author this morning. Loraine and I were disporting ourselves in a rough sea when the tide turned just as I had exhausted myself diving through breakers; and I was carried out helpless and swept along to the north. Loraine found himself in the same predicament. Our attempts to swim in were useless: the harder we tried the further out we were; and as out of every ten waves, at least 7, 8. 9. and 10 snowed us under in boiling froth, we gave up all idea of getting out of it alive in spite of our involuntary efforts to drink the bay dry. However, when we were utterly done the tide carried us on a spit of shoal; and here we are, none the worse.

In haste to catch post.
G.B.S.

Ellen Terry had been touring Captain Brassbound's Conversion *in the provinces after a tour of the play in America. She was coming to London and proposed to bring the play into the West End. Vedrenne and Barker objected to this but Shaw would not listen to them. Johnston Forbes-Robertson was to bring his production of* Caesar and Cleopatra *to the Savoy, which did not please Barker. Shaw on holiday in Wales had paid a visit to* You Never Can Tell *on tour and communicates his horror at the performance to Barker, who was responsible for the management. Vedrenne was to open his new theatre in Shaftesbury Avenue in October—he called it not the Central but the Queen's. Barker's* Waste *is referred to; it had not yet been censored. Essie is the little girl in* The Devil's Disciple *and Thyza Norman was the divorced wife of J. H. Leigh. Shaw's new play was* Getting Married; *it is easy to see how the theme was suggested to him. The guarantee fund was to be for the Savoy management. The antagonistic attitude of Shaw to the Restoration dramatists is defined; he had other reasons for keeping Barker off Shakespeare. This letter is written in indelible pencil on ruled paper taken from an exercise book.*

Llanbedr, Merioneth.
7th September 1907.

As to Brassbound, I have written to Ellen and to Courtenay pointing out the unlikeliness of any good coming of three weeks at the Apollo, with Society out of town, immediately following four weeks in the suburbs. But if she chooses to let Davis empty her pockets, which are being fairly filled by the tour (she draws £100 a night pretty steadily) why should I stop her? You say you and Vedrenne would rather I did; but I dare say you had rather also that Bouchier, Maude, Tree, Harrison and Frohman would close their theatres and leave the field to you. Have you noticed that for about a year past you and V.D. have been capable of any crime. The £200 to Hankin was the penalty for pure crime—deliberate, intentional crime for the sake of crime. One of my assets this winter will be Caesar and Cleopatra in my native city—involving £100 tentieres for me. V.D. actually persuaded Forbes-Robertson to throw me over solely because he thought the scenery would look newer at the Savoy if it was not shipped to Ireland. Of course I very promptly persuaded F.R. back again; but do you realise the colossal selfishness of the transaction? And now you calmly intimate that if I have any delicacy I will refuse to let the leading lady of the British stage appear in Brassbound in a West End Theatre—for my own good, of course.

Have you any conscience left—any sense of proportion—any touch with the universe outside King Street?

And this, mind, at a moment when you are openly preparing to throw V.D. over, and he is actually throwing you over, and it looks as if my plays will be homeless in London in 18 months time!

I motored over to Aberystwyth to see You Never Can Tell—Casson's suggestion. The faithful ghastly Towers epitomized in his countenance the impression of the performance. The materials were there for a quite tolerable cast: but the invincible recalcitrance of the management undid the kindness of Fortune. With Mary Hamilton there actually on the stage, Miss Lambourn, every inch a well-behaved matron, was cast for Dolly. She was promised her chance, was little Mary; and this is how she gets it. Oh Italian traitor, who shall be loyal to thee? Little Dorrit—Amy—grown larger than her husband, and exhibited as a barelegged columbine! Penelope, earnestly stupid, made Mrs. Clandon a Burne-Jonesian aesthete and missed every point in the part with intense assiduity. She would have been quite possible as Gloria; but that would have involved the concession to the author of casting Mary Barton for Mrs. Clandon, which she would have looked and played very well. She played Gloria like a rusty lawn mower. Valentine made wierd effects by taking every passage he did not understand as an outburst of raving lunacy. Gwenn gave a spirited performance of Quersimode, the hunchback of Notre Dame, to my words, and was voted the best of the lot by our chauffeur. He underlined every comma and rammed in his points without surface, without delicacy, without decency. Lowe was quite imposing as McComas; Page's squalor as the harlequin would have disgraced a penny gaff (cant you buy him something second hand, or at least get his hat pipeclayed?); and Gurney was, on the whole, the star of the tour.

You will observe that what was wrong was the management. The play is actor-proof fortunately: if it were not, the tour would have ended weeks ago in some harbor at low water among the dead fish.

And you have the audacity to criticise Ellen's crowd! You make a compliment of accepting Forbes Robertson's! For Heaven's sake bring Mrs. Page back to London to understudy Judith (the only part of mine she is any use for); make Penelope and Mary Barton change parts; turn Mary Hamilton loose as Dolly; and dress Page decently.

If you do not play Burgoyne Lablache had better. But quality for quality nobody will be so cheap as you; so V.D. had better stick to you. Who is going to play Medea? Janet is down here clashing a new set of teeth like castanets, and very wild, wierd and game for anything.

What V. & B. want is a great moral regeneration. Vedrenne is definitely mad: he sent a play down here to Loraine which only extreme intoxication could have reconciled Martin Harvey to, and which Loraine couldnt have played at all—a fearful product of actor-authorship; and V.D. actually believes there is money in it. The papers say he is going to call his theatre the Central, as if it were a Criminal Court or a railway terminus. We should call it the BravoHicks to distinguish it from the Hicks. Both you and he are getting softening of the brain—each of you "a fellow almost damned in a fair wife."

I have just been reading Hankin's Three Plays With Happy Endings: and Cassilis is splendid.

You had better send me Waste and let me cast it. I no longer trust you for anything.

V.D. says you have cast Thyza Norman for Essie. Bigamy will be the next move. I had hopes that Lion Phillimore would have devoured you, and Lillah taken Bobby as a hors d'oeuvre, with a general wreck of this demoralizing domesticity as a result. I should make Lillah elope with me if I had the faintest idea of what I should do with her afterwards. Nothing destroys character like love making.

I have not since the first day written a line of the new play; and I dont believe it will be ready until Autumn 1908.

It took me a whole day to draw up an agreement for that guarantee fund. In it I expressly bar Congreve and Shakespear; but The Merry Wives or Henry IV with Chesterton as Falstaff might soften me on this point.

How soon do you want super dialogue for The Devil's Disciple? Ask Miss Dewar to send me a calendar with dates of rehearsals as well as productions.

Yrs ever
G.B.S.

The Savoy season opened on 16 September with Shaw's You Never Can Tell *produced by Barker. The changed atmosphere of the management was evidenced by playing the National Anthem in the conventional way, which horrified Shaw, as he declares. A. E. George had the part of Crampton. Lillah McCarthy did not play Medea. "Joy" was John Galsworthy's play done at the Savoy on 24th September. This is another important letter for the variety of subjects referred to in it.*

Hafody Bryn, Llanbedr, Merionethshire. R.S.O.
18th Sept. 1907.

I learn with disgust and horror that you played the National Anthem and made the audience stand up on Monday. I ask you: is Y.N.C.T. a pantomime? Is the Savoy Drury Lane? Is Stier Glover? Have you any notion of the extent to which your sworn supporters are republicans or aristocratic souls with a loathing for public demonstrations? A hideous solecism—a symptom of vital decay—of pothouse politics. Shame!

Also I note your determination to suppress cheap actors. You chuck poor underpriced Gurney from the Savoy because he is wanted for the tour. Then you drop him out of the tour quietly, and fill your soul with the joy of paying an extra £5. a week to George, who will just miss the injured pathos of Crampton.

Better have put another £10 on to Mrs. Clandon, who will just make all the difference. Oh G.B. you are a very clever and interesting youth of 30; but you are an atrocious manager. You dont know where to put your high light, and where to put your smudge.

However, my main interest in this letter is Medea. If Lillah is to play that Matron, you must get Ricketts to do a dress for her that will make her a picture. If she appears as a real woman she will be offered Mrs. Hardcastle or the Nurse in R. & J. next week. You must get her on the fantastic plane, and handle the play accordingly. The great impression of Dona Ann must be nursed.

The Webbs think Waste good. I will not do a new play for this season: I dont see why Joy and Waste should not take up the running, with perhaps a revival of Barbara to fill up a bit. The thing to aim at now is a season without a single Shaw evening bill. Every night of Shaw is now time lost: I am not going to sit down in the way I have cleared, and block it.

Caesar seems to have waked up Leeds. Yesterday was thick with reply-paid telegrams from the local papers (to be exact, two).

I have not told Trebitsch that his play is rejected; the news must wait until his nerves are cured. Nora Charrington, who wants to go on the stage, has lately become very good-looking—worth keeping an eye on. Hankin is full of commissions, it seems. Charrington plays Sartorius in Manchester: Janet something by Calman (!) chez Flanagan.

G.B.S.

The play referred to in the following was Barker's production of You Never Can Tell *and this brief note contains a criticism of Barker's methods as a producer.*

Hafody Bryn, Llanbedr, Merionethshire. R.S.O.
19th Sept. 1907.

Your letter crossed mine. I should have come up for the last few rehearsals: the combination works better than the single cylinder. You are so afraid of their acting badly that you make them afraid too. And you exhaust yourself over the job until you have no oxygen to turn on at the end. However, a bit of training does them no harm, it will enable me to let them rip all the more recklessly next time. Try and make George look puzzled and injured, if he can. That was what was so good about Gurney: he seemed to be in chronic wounded surprise because everybody didnt love him at first sight.

G.B.S.

Shaw's desperate interest in everything done at the Savoy is shown in his comment on the choice of Edyth Olive for Medea. *But the point of the next letter is that Forbes-Robertson intended to bring* Caesar and Cleopatra *to the Coronet Theatre at Notting Hill, before coming to the Savoy in November. Also there was trouble with Vedrenne and Lillah, for Vedrenne set his face against her playing, which was largely Shaw's fault. Among the plays Vedrenne had rejected altogether was John Masefield's* Nan *because Lillah was to play the leading part. This was a considerable error. Phyllis in the following letter was Mrs. Vedrenne. It is evident that Shaw was letting Barker produce his plays. He had been talking about* Getting Married, *which was completed the following year.*

Hafody Bryn, Llanbedr, Merionethshire. R.S.O.
23rd Sept. 1907.

Dear Barker,

If it was only Weber's blessed old Jubal overture, then we may overlook it and applaud the wiliness of Renard Vedrenne Esq., who of course knew all about it. He is after a knighthood, is M.C. Vieux Renard: it is not for nothing that he has called his theatre the Queen's—though why not the Alexandra?

I knew it would be Edyth Olive. If only there was a little less of the part, a sort of a kind of effect—but what's the use of talking?

Vedrenne's habit of calling people by their Christian names will be his ruin. When you do that, how can you refuse to engage them? and oh! that habit of doing everything three times over. In future we must really make casts and stick to them.

Otherwise we shall have all King Street on the salary list eating their heads off.

Charlotte has just got Forbes-Robertson's itinerary; and the third item in it is a crushing blow to us. My one iron stipulation was that Caesar was not to come to London until it came to the Savoy; and now behold! Sept. 23 to Sept. 28, the CORONET THEATRE W!!!! V.D. assured me that this was not dreamt of. Now we are done for. All we have is a revival. The Coronet is as much a West End Theatre as the Court. All the critics will go: all the notices will appear: all our special clientele will jump at the low prices. And it is too late to do anything. The 23rd is *tonight*. Well, I shall get my percentage at the Coronet, same's at the Savoy; but it's not my doing. I called attention to the danger; I was told not to excite myself—that no such thing was contemplated; I didn't excite myself; and this—THIS, G.B. is the result. Well, Kismet! V.D. had better play Burgoyne, I think, and hand over the office to me. Let us hope that since revivals pay better than original performances with us—but they DONT: my first six matinees mean the cream of the adventure; and the Coronet is skimming it.

This feud between V.D. and Lillah is beyond my powers of management. Short of giving Phyllis a leading part, and thus giving you the hammer lock on him, I dont know what to do. Dont quarrel about it anyhow and dont argue about it. Tell him that you submit to an unprovoked injury as the price of his friendship.

Charlotte leaves for Ireland tomorrow (Tuesday) afternoon. I shall hold on here until Friday or Saturday. As there is an offchance of my being up for Saturday, tell them to start sending me rehearsal calls on that day. I am fearfully rushed, having three long affairs to write before I leave, and Trebitsch's Perfect Wagnerite to read through (or finish reading through) in double Dutch before I leave, besides packing and one or two overhanging jobs that I am despairingly letting slide. Nevertheless send Waste. When Trebitsch is off my mind I can read it after dinner, and be ready to cast it when I get back to my list.

I suppose I must take John Bull in hand and leave you to bend all your energies on the D's D. I do not intend to interfere really with that, except to produce an effect of upsetting everything at the end, if it seems firm enough to stand that treatment.

Is Kennedy a possible Undershaft, or Harcourt Williams a possible Charteris? H. W.'s Orestes and Romeo convinced me that he was a born comedian; and the papers speak well of him as Valentine; but I suspend judgement until I have seen Y.N.C.T. which will perhaps occur on Saturday night. Keep a box for me unless somebody wants to buy it, in which case another night will serve.

I seriously dont think I will write the Marriage play yet. It will improve by keeping; and I must make some sort of clearance of arrears of other things.

G.B.S.

Hafody Bryn, Llanbedr, Merionethshire. R.S.O.
25th Sept. 1907.

Of course, now I remember—that was why V.D. told me not to excite myself. Excitement subsided accordingly.

Am sending for copy of D's. D. Will try to do some crowd dialogue on Saturday in the train.

The 5 train on Saturday is quite impossible: it looks more like the 9.40-11.5 on Sunday morning.

Waste received. Why do you write on blankets? handkerchiefs are large enough.

G.B.S.

Barker had sent Shaw the manuscript of his new play Waste. *He had a habit of writing on large sheets of paper in large handwriting. In the following letter Shaw mentions a visit he intends to make to the Barkers:*

Hafody Bryn, Llanbedr, Merionethshire. R.S.O.
27th Sept. 1907.

At best—if it is fine enough for me to cycle to Barmouth and catch the 10.15 train there, I shall not reach Paddington until 5.20 and I shall not then want any more railway that evening. So I will go to Y.N.C.T. and catch the 9.40-11.5 to Haslemere on Sunday morning. I shall reduce my kit to a minimum and walk from Haslemere to Fernhurst if it is fine. It would do you a lot of good to come and meet me instead of working.

The copy of Waste is very inaccurate—full of holes in the text. I dont think it will be difficut to cast: it will play itself if the people are at all plausible.

We can leave the rehearsal question open until we meet, as there is no hurry for a day or two.

G.B.S.

Shaw wrote to Vedrenne on 26 October sending him a cheque, "This leaves me stony," and a week later he wrote to Forbes-Robertson to say—

. . . the pit, gallery, upper circle and half the balcony are sticking to us nobly: the deficiency is in the stalls . . .

It was intended that Barker's Waste should follow in the evening bill, and it was announced for 19th November; but a blow fell on the management, and upon Barker in particular, for the Censor of Plays refused to pass it. In particular the omission of a reference to a criminal operation was insisted upon, to which Barker would not agree. This was a painful disappointment, for Barker placed great hopes upon the play, which was thought highly of by those who had read it. John Masefield wrote to him "It is the only modern English play which has made me feel, as all ought to make one feel, that I have been in the presence of a law giver." Shaw's judgement was "Waste is superb."

The casting of Arms and the Man was in hand and Shaw was determined to have Lillah. He intended to overcome Vedrenne's opposition by getting her at a salary much below her usual rate, which he considered would appeal to the business man. He wrote artfully to Barker:

Ayot St. Lawrence, Welwyn, Herts.
17th November 1907.

PRIVATE. Not to be communicated to Lillah on any account. The other night at the D's. D. when Arnold Lucy was having a rare beano as Swindon, Charlotte said that she had often noticed that in my plays any part, however apparently insignificant, could become the principal one if it got into the right hands.

I suppose, after this, you will not mind playing Octavius, vice Casson transferred to Manchester.

However, that is not the great treachery now about to be whispered. How far is it possible for Sergius and Louka to shift the centre of levity from (bother! cant spell it)—from Blunt Chilly and Raina to themselves, or at least to make themselves a centre of gravity in contrast? Strictly between our guilty selves, if I can get Lillah into the play to walk in beauty like the night. I do not care a twopenny—or say a tenpenny—damn what she plays. She can play Raina on her head; but so can anybody. She doesnt like playing with the ice eyed Bobby, who will simply play off her as if she were a concrete wall at rackets; and she plays very magically with you. Edith Wynne-Matthison can play Raina at 12 hours notice, with less color and blood than Lillah, but to perfection for Loraine's purposes and her own. It is in Louka that one wants color and blood. Suppose Lillah were to play Louka to your Sergius!! It is in tradition for Louka to be the manageress' part; and Sergius is to be the manager. The question is, dare you, as a married man, propose it? To me the scenes between Sergius and Louka are so much more deeply felt than those between Bluntschli and Raina that I had myself rather play Sergius than Bluntschli, and rather have the strong woman of the cast as my Louka than as my Raina; but I know that this is not how it would strike most leading ladies. Just think over it before we commit ourselves to Auriol Lee, who will drop a little vinegar into your cup. She could play Violet, by the way, and Sylvia in The Philanderer—cant she?

G.B.S.

Barker played Sergius when the play was done, but Lillah, of course, was not moved from the leading part, despite Shaw's mischievous suggestion. Waste was privately performed by the Stage Society at the Imperial Theatre on 24 November, when Barker had to play the leading part at the last moment. On the following 28 January at 11 a.m. at the Savoy, a copyright performance took place with the passages objected to by the censor deleted, the parts being played by Bernard Shaw, Mrs. Shaw, Mr. & Mrs. H. G. Wells, John Galsworthy, St. John Hankin, William Archer, Allan Wade and other friends of the author, and though Gilbert Murray's name appeared in the cast he was not able to be present.

Johnston Forbes-Robertson brought Caesar and Cleopatra to the Savoy on 25 November. This interrupted the Vedrenne-Barker season for five weeks, and The Devil's Disciple was transferred to the Queen's, Barker taking over the part of Dick Dudgeon. Shaw had written the Caesar play for Forbes-Robertson in 1898, the one classic actor of his time in Shaw's opinion, and the part of Cleopatra was for Mrs. Patrick Campbell. The latter gave the copyright performance in Newcastle-on-Tyne on 15 March 1899, but did not play in it. It was characteristic of Shaw that when at last in December 1903 Forbes-Robertson had the idea of producing the play, Shaw put him off, telling him that it was to be done "with great splendour at the Neues Theatre in Berlin in February", and that it would cost a lot of money to dress and was very difficult to cast. It was however announced by the Stage Society that a performance of the first act of the play would be given by Forbes-Robertson in September 1903, which did not eventualize.

Forbes-Robertson tried again in 1905, proposing to perform it in New York, but Shaw would not let him do so unless he rehearsed the company himself, so that was done, and the play was first produced at the New Amsterdam Theatre in New York, on 29 October 1906. Pressed to go to the first performance Shaw refused saying that if he were to go to America "I should become so popular that they'd want to make me President." Eleven months later Forbes-Robertson brought the production to England and gave the first performance in this country at the Grand Theatre, Leeds, on 16 September 1907. He took the play on tour and the five weeks at the Savoy followed. The programme stated: "The part of Julius Caesar was written expressly for Mr. Forbes-Robertson and the interpretation of the play was directed by him in consultation with the Author."

The London season was not a financial success. In fact the production was nowhere near the Vedrenne-Barker standard. There was some question about Shaw and Barker going together to see a performance before it came to the Savoy, for Barker wanted to persuade Shaw that it was not good enough, but Shaw wrote to Forbes-Robertson telling him of the suggestion and their decision not to act upon it, saying "You are a sufficiently presentable actor to be able to appear without supervision in a theatre made classic by the illustrious traditions of Vedrenne-Barker and Bernard Shaw. But I thought on the whole I would chance it". It was not so much that Forbes-Robertson himself was lacking as that the weakness of a company engaged for tours made the Savoy management rightly apprehensive. At the end of the season Shaw wrote to the actor ". . . away with it, and forgive the author. He meant well". Forbes-Robertson was so pleased, however, that he included the play in his farewell season at Drury Lane in 1913.

Shaw wrote several letters to Vedrenne about the production of Arms and the Man that have survived. On November 22 he wrote:

I have swindled Lillah into accepting a percentage of 2½ over £150 in lieu of her loss by taking £20. That's the most I can do, as Barker knows I am cheating her and is furious about it.

Two days later he writes:

The lady agrees for the three plays at £25. Oh be joyful.

And on 12 December he says that Lillah is to have a contract for £25. for an engagement of twelve weeks from 30 December. Her dresses for Arms and the Man are to be provided by the management from the designs of Charles Ricketts, and she is to have £60 for dressing Ann Whitefield, and £50 for dressing Julia, if she plays those parts, which she did not.

The play was well received, and was, indeed, a fine production. "It is a brilliant thing, this play," wrote Max Beerbohm; "but shrill in tone and narrow in outlook, and shallow, as compared with the work of Mr. Shaw in his maturity." Loraine himself said of it:

"When we play Arms and the Man half the house is amused and

half the house is furious; but all the house is incredulous of one point—a soldier eating chocolate. Yet what else did we survive on in the Boer War, and what else did Queen Victoria send as the most suitable Christmas Gift to her soldiers in the field in 1900?"

Miss McCarthy did not like her part because she did not care for playing with Loraine. *As she says in her memoirs* Myself and My Friends, *she and Shaw "came nearer to disagreement over Raina than ever we had done before or have done since." Shaw told her that she "must feed Bluntschli very carefully . . . and you must take care to caracole very proudly indeed every time a fall is coming." He was displeased with her performance, saying "Raina has gone to bits. You play the part unstilted all through and the effect is disastrous. Robert Loraine is playing you off the stage . . . he has found out how to drive the play through without you . . . You never pay the slightest attention to him . . . If I were he, I would give you a yell of rage, seize you by the ankles and swing you round my head and let you fly into the pit, and rush screaming from the theatre." He was daring her to ride the high horse, and she did so for that letter, and did so afterwards in the play. At the end of the run, however, she was ill.*

Charles Ricketts *wrote to her some years later:*
"Concerning Arms and the Man *I have nothing to say save in praise of a superb all round performance, my contribution being confined to your two dresses. This was the first occasion when the bustle was revived on the stage, today no Cochran revue can do without it. I think, at the time, you were a little frightened. Shaw rather neutral, but when worn by you this fashion proved so charming that its success was immediate with the Char Ladies who were dusting during the rehearsal. 'Aint She lovely,' they exclaimed and I have ever since considered the employees of a theatre the soundest judges of scenery and dresses."*

As a curtain raiser Frederick Fenn's The Convict on the Hearth *was revived, one of the last appearances of a first piece in the West End of London. "First pieces" were not, however, continued at the Savoy. Shaw wrote to show his pleasure at the treatment of his play.*

Edstaston, Wem.
Jan. 2 1908.

The weather here is very bright and very cold. Motor transit went without a hitch. Charlotte at a farmers' ordinary at Towcester was immense.

I think it would be nice of us to send seats for Arms and the Man to C. T. H. Helmsley and Florence Farr. Helmsley was the ostensible manager of the 1894 production.

There is Dr. Louis Elkind, 4 Park Place, St. James's, S.W. who is writing articles on the Kaiser in the English reviews and on the English stage for the German papers, who might fill up a couple of seats with profit when there are any to spare. He is keen on G.B. and G.B.S.

All notices that I have seen have praised the cast of Arms to the skies. If it doesn't pay, nothing will. Loraine wants to know when we begin rehearsing again.

G.B.S.

Loraine was thinking about the projected revival of Man and Superman. *The dramatist referred to in the following letter, Norreys Connell, the pen name of Conal O'Riordan, was associated with the Irish National Theatre Society. He wrote a number of plays, and afterwards had much success as a novelist.*

10, Adelphi Terrace,
London W.C.
11th January 1908.

Dear Barker,

There is a little play by Norreys Connell, called Woman to Woman, which I believe you have got. I am now told that the Stage Society want a first piece and that they have asked him for it. He says you have got it, and that he cannot get it out of you or any information concerning it. As we seem to want first pieces at The Savoy, you had better know what is up. Why dont you send the man back his play if you are not going to do it? If it is the thing he read out to me—a scene in a hotel in Paris—it ought to be treated with proper respect.

We got back yesterday afternoon after doing the ninety miles from Broadway in a nipping and an eager air. I think I am now going to have a headache. Probably I shall spent next week at Ayot, as there seems nothing to come up for.

March, with it equinoctial gales, is quite the liveliest time for crossing the Atlantic. But what go you out for to see?

I can no more. The hysterical yawnings which preclude a headache make it impossible for me to go on.

Love to Lillah.

Yours ever,
G.B.S.

Tuesday afternoon and headache over. Shall be up for a moment tomorrow afternoon to attend S. S. Committee (or perhaps I will) but shall return forthwith, as there are no Fabian committees this week. Pease being away at the Annual Conference of the I.L.P. at Hull.

Here is Shaw telling Barker off in his usual style. The play was The Philanderer, *which Shaw never ceased to urge should be given a production, with Barker resisting. It was not, however, revived. Rosina Filippi was playing Catherine in* Arms and the Man.

Ayot St. Lawrence, Welwyn, Herts.
19th January 1908.

Granville Barker,

When will you understand that what has ruined you as a manager is your love for people who are "a little weak, perhaps, but just the right tone." The right tone is never a little weak perhaps; it is always devastatingly strong. Keep your worms for your own plays; and leave me the drunken, stagey, brassbowelled barnstormers my plays are written for.

Can we get Ellen O'Malley for Grace? If we cant get Lewis for the Colonel, we shall have to get either Sherbrooke or Nigel Playfair. I *must* have people who can say a thing as if they meant it. Hearn can play Paramore.

If we can get Lewis, there is just half a chink of an open question about reviving the Doctor's Dilemma; but with Loraine and Lillah I think the Phil. is strongly indicated. Lillah would score enormously on an anticipation of failure for the part.

Rosine, bless her, must be allowed one night a week for the distractions of which Charlotte has always suspected her. However, we can always fall back on Mrs. Theodore, Fanny Brough or Geraldine Oliffe. Tell Bowyer to look after the entrances, or put on a special man and stop his wages out of her salary.

I shall come up early tomorrow and lunch at Adelphi Terrace. I dare not ask a formal guest, as waiting at table is not in Mrs. Bilton's contract; but she regards you as a son, so if you look in at 1.30 you can be fed.

G.B.S.

The letter to the weekly newspaper, The Nation, *was about the performance of the censored* Waste. *The matinees of the play with the text altered to suit the censor were never done, apart from the copyright performance, for Barker would not budge.*

Ayot St. Lawrence, Welwyn,Herts.

31st Jan. 1908.

Massingham says my letter is late for this week's Nation and must wait until next. He considers it a smasher for G.A.R.

Dont you think that now parliament is sitting and we still have a theatre on hand, you had better put up some matinees of Waste. There would be nothing extra for rent: our clientele would all come over again, plus the political people; and you could put a note in the program to say that the poison alteration is at the request of the Lord C. The matinees would pay.

We shall be up on Monday and Tuesday—here until then.

G.B.S.

Gilbert Cannan, who is mentioned below, was twenty-four at this date, a Lancashire man who had offered a play to Barker. He became an unfriendly critic of Barker, and ran off with J. M. Barrie's wife. He wrote a number of plays produced at the Birmingham Repertory Theatre and elsewhere.

Ayot St. Lawrence, Welwyn, Herts.
7th Feb. 1908.

Cannan must do better than F. & S. if we are to spend all that money on producing it. It is very promising; but it is too boyish to offer to grown-up people. There are limits even to the encouragement of the young. It is like Kipling's boy imitating his parent.

Calvert as Straker is not a happy idea. Tony Weller, yes. As Enry Straker, no. Tomorrow letters of mine will probably appear in The Nation (Censorship), The Saturday Review (Regicide) & The Daily News (Blasphemy). And I am expected to write plays! Also to Lillah.

Playfair will end by doing a Milward tour of Candida. He is hard at it.

See Teleki. I do not feel convinced that he has either the god-like qualities you desiderate; but I have ground him to powder and then made him my agent for Hungary. See him: there is pathos in Teleki.

A tour of Arms and The Man *was being discussed, and Shaw was, as ever, in militant mood. "K.M." was Kenyon Musgrave. There was a suggestion to buy the Court Theatre. The Tree scheme was the After Noon Theatre at His Majesty's, an imitation of the Vedrenne-Barker matinees.*

Ayot St. Lawrence, Welwyn, Herts.
10th March 1908.

Imprimis, the lunch tomorrow is off, as I am not coming up until the afternoon. I shall be at Clements Inn at 5.20 (about) for a Propaganda Committee. Come to dinner at 7.30, or else see me after the committee. A line by return will reach me before I leave. If we hear nothing from you we will expect you to dinner.

K.M. substituted for Barnes means that the wrath of the Life Force has gathered on V. & B. and is driving them to their doom. Why not Lloyd instead of K.M.? Why not the baggage man instead of Lloyd? He would be a saving, as far as salary goes.

There was a man though some did think him mad,
The more he gave away, the more he had.

Bunyan.

Go: give to Barnes and all the rest double what they ask, and do not spoil the provincial ship for a haporth of tar.

As to Petkoff, I want Sherbrooke. But, failing him, can Haigh play Petkoff. Surely these two character parts are the obvious ones to fit with one man. Sherbrooke could play Straker if it came to that, though his Board School would have to be the Ghetto, Budapest.

I enclose a letter from Sidney Thompson, once a brilliant London critic (musical—on the old resplendent Star) who calmly asks for a box. I wont buy a box for him. If you think him worth bribing, poor fellow, and have an empty box, bribe him by all means.

Let Cannan send in his wretched play. He can write one if he likes—or will grow into it presently.

Let the Court wait. If it is snapped up, so much the better: we shall do without it. If not, it will be all the cheaper for not having been snapped up. Take no thought for the autumn: it is the present season that we must live through.

The Tree scheme is utter rot. WHY should he be in it? ? ?

G.B.S.

When the Savoy tenancy was ending Barker paid the rather long delayed visit to New York, taking William Archer with him, but he found the new theatre he had been asked to direct much too large for the kind of work he wanted to do, which was to conduct a repertory theatre, so that he turned down the proposal and returned at once to London. During his absence Vedrenne and Shaw had been negotiating with Frederick Harrison, lessee and manager of the Theatre Royal, Haymarket, for the production of Shaw's new play, the first for two years, Getting Married, *also Laurence Housman and Joseph Moorant's new piece,* The Chinese Lantern, *and possibly other plays. Like other intelligent managers, Harrison was interested in the possibilities of the new*

drama, and wanted to be in the movement. He had,
contemplated doing Arms and the Man *as long before as*
1906, when the Court Theatre was in full swing, as w
from a letter from Shaw to Vedrenne dated the 10th
month:

I have found Harrison's letter here waiting for me. He
Hawtry to play Bluntschli. All there is to be said for the pr
is that *Arms and the Man* needs a cast of expensive stars of
fashionable kind. But I don't see my way at present to let
it go unless you or Barker have formed any plans which invo
discarding it as a possibility at the Court.

As usual Shaw gave attention to every detail of the productio
of the new play at the Haymarket as his letters to Vedrenn
indicate. He was anxious that Barker should play the Bishop
but Barker would not take it, and Shaw's second choice was
Ainley. He prepared a sketch for the setting, described the
costumes, indicated the incidental music, and even discussed
the box office management, the programmes and bills. On a draft
of the bill he put the author's name in minute characters. In the
Enthoven Collection at the Victoria and Albert Museum there
are two note books filled with shorthand notes by Shaw made
at the rehearsals. There are also notes in longhand on sheets of
green paper about the acting.

Ayot St. Lawrence.
3rd April 1908 (Sat. 9.45 a.m.)
This in great haste. Charlotte is going up by the 10.47 train
and must take this to post in London.

Vedrenne and Barker, though dead, yet live. The Daily Telegraph has announced my new play for production at the Haymarket (Mr. Frederick Harrison presents the Brothers V. & B.
in a new and thrilling &c. &c) on the 12th. May or thereabouts
for matinees, and the evening bill (with matinees of the Chinese
Lantern—though this is not announced) on the 8th. June, or
sooner if Mrs. Langtry can be bought out; the cast is practically

settled and all the leading artists engaged; the contract with Harrison is signed (pig in a poke so far as the play goes); and the postman staggers under bags of letters asking me for parts.

All this has depended on force majeure at the centre. The alternative proposals were (a) get rid of the superfluous Vedrenne, (b) get rid of the intolerable Barker, or (c) get rid of both Vedrenne and Barker, those notorious incompetent muddlers and amateurs. Fate (whose initials are G.B.S.) decreed that nobody should be got rid of, and that the old amateur muddling should go on.

V.D. has worked hard and organized the production. He will probably put it to you whether, as a gentleman, you can ask for a salary when you have been doing nothing but razzling in America. Your reply is that *I* am doing your work, i.e. producing the play, and that you are ready to take it up at a moment's notice when you are wanted. You will have, for instance, to light the lantern. Hand your salary over to me by all means if you like, *but draw it*.

This tides us over the summer season, and gives a starlighting smack in the eye to the chorus who were hypocritically lamenting that John Barleycorn was dead. The rebound is already apparent and will presently be extreme.

Later on, the future can be considered in view of the report you bring up from the land of Canaan. At present Harrison is ready to give three months a year to the new drama.

It is important that the Chinese Lantern or some other *new* play should be produced by V. & B. at the Haymarket this time; if only for matinees; so as to make the affair really a V. B. season and not a West End production of a play by me.

I shall get no holiday. That means the rest of the year in an asylum.

Charlotte's cab approaches.

G.B.S.

P.S. The quantity of public and private lying that the above arrangements have involved (quite unnecessarily) is beyond belief.

P.S.S. Candida will be produced at the Theatre des Arts in April. Paris will capitulate ten years later.

Announced as "Mr. Frederick Harrison's and Messrs. Vedrenne and Barker's series of Vedrenne-Barker Matinees," Getting Married *was performed on 12 May 1908 with a cast including Robert Loraine, Henry Ainley, Mary Rorke, Marie Lohr, Auriol Lee, Edith Craig, and Fanny Brough, one of the best companies ever got together for a Shaw play. He called it flatly "a discussion" to anticipate the objection of the critics that it was not a play, and to emphasise his theory of drama. Originally it was described as "an instructive conversation in one piece." When published its sub-title was "a disquisitory play." The piece was written in the manner of "classic" drama, the dramatic unities of time, place and action strictly observed. The author set out deliberately to assault the dramatic critics. Five days prior to the first performance he gave a long interview to the* Daily Telegraph *in which he declared that he was going to be revenged upon the critics for:*

". . . their arrant Philistinism, their shameless intellectual laziness, their low tastes, their hatred of good work, their puerile romanticism, their disloyalty to dramatic literature, their stupendous ignorance, their insensibility to honour, virtue, intellectual honesty, and anything that constitutes strength and dignity in human character—in short, for all the vices and follies and weaknesses of which Vedrenne and Barker have been trying to cure them for four years past."

The long discussion of which they had complained in Don Juan in Hell, *which lasted only 110 minutes, was, he said, to be stretched out to 150 minutes:*

"There will be no costumes by Mr. Ricketts—nothing but a bishop in an apron. There will be no music by Mr. Theodore Stier or Mozart or anyone else. There will be nothing but talk, talk, talk, talk, talk,—Shaw talk. The characters will seem to the wretched critics to be simply a row of Shaws, all arguing with one another on totally uninteresting subjects . . . The whole thing will be hideous, indescribable—an eternity of brain-racking dullness. And yet they will have to sit it out."

When asked if he had deliberately written a bad play in order to make the critics suffer, he declared:

121

"Good heavens, no . . . I have deliberately written a good play, that is the way to make the Press suffer."

The interview was so well written that there can be little doubt that Shaw wrote it himself.

Of course, the critics fell upon him. Shaw's friend and candid critic, J. T. Grein, wrote in dire pain:

". . . the peculiar weaknesses of Shaw are glaringly manifest in it. His loquacity is literally torrential . . . the hearer's mind is taxed to over-straining."

Even Max Beerbohm said that "the fun does not seem to be integral: it seems to have been foisted in, for fear lest we should fidget." The Daily Telegraph itself gave a long and detailed notice, finding the first two hours "exceedingly bright and amusing . . . the interest is kept up with no small measure of success," but the last act "chills our interest and sends us out of the theatre a little perplexed and more than a little bored." But the critic thought the piece "admirably acted."

Shaw wrote to Vedrenne ten days after the first performance:

The cast finds out more every time what it is all about: and so, consequently, does the audience. It just wants to be made an hour longer and played every day for the next ten years . . . All that the play wants is £10,000 to nurse it into a full grown institution.

He was convinced that it was necessary only to hold on and the public would be brought round to perceive the play's merits.

Although said to indicate a falling off of the dramatist's powers, the play was in fact a tour de force, and an admirable stage work, as subsequent revivals have shown. On 8 June it was put into the evening bill where it continued until the middle of the following month.

In the meantime, John Masefield's second play, The Tragedy of Nan, had had a series of matinees starting on 2 June after a performance the previous Sunday evening at the Royalty Theatre by the actors' play-producing society, The Pioneers. Barker produced it, and Lillah McCarthy in the name part had one of her most admired characters. Shaw was insistent upon doing this play *though Vedrenne was emphatically against it, but, as Shaw warned him, he was driving Barker out of the partnership, and he gave way. Masefield wrote to Barker while the play was being rehearsed:*

"You must not go spending your vitality on Nan, let the baggage go hang. I am ashamed to think that Nan may have kept you from writing."

Miss McCarthy had been seriously ill after Arms and the Man *at the Savoy; she had to go away for a holiday. Her performance in Masefield's play delighted the dramatist, as it did all who saw it.*

The long expected Housman-Moorant musical play, The Chinese Lantern, *started eight matinees on 16 June. It was not a success. Indeed this final Vedrenne-Barker season was far from being financially rewarding, though* Getting Married *and* Nan *were dramatic achievements. It cost Shaw a good deal. He wrote to Vedrenne the day before his letter of 1 July to Barker:*

The enclosed makes £1000 which the Haymarket scheme has cost me less £300. fees, and plus the value of my time spent on rehearsing. I am quite of Mrs. George's opinion. It is enough. I can go no further. It is much too much . . . As it is I am a poorer and not in the least a wiser man.

In fact the partners were in great disharmony at this time and Shaw himself was the only enthusiast.

The troublesome Fanny Brough, who played Mrs. George, was certainly splendid in Shaw's play. Frances Dillon first appeared on the stage in 1895 and played many leading parts. She was engaged for Ann Whitefield and toured in Man and Superman: *she also played Louka in* Arms and the Man *on tour.*

10 Adelphi Terrace, W.C.
17th June 1908.

Matinee of Lantern today £23! G.M. last night £120 odd. Strain on V. and H. of taking off G.M. and putting on C.L. correspondingly severe. V. says if H. wants this done, he must pay the C.L. salaries. Tragedy yesterday at matinee. Archer left after a few minutes of Act III. Mrs. G. having put an enemy into her mouth. Thrilling subsequent scene with V. Mrs. G. imprisoned by his orders for five hours with soda water and strict diet. Result— when I went over at 10 to see Auriol Lee take her place—F.B. absolutely at her best: a splendid performance.

However, this is anecdote, not business. Stella writes to say "if mother doesnt go on tour we are remaining in London this autumn"! This is not good enough. I saw Frances Dillon this morning, and collapsed at the first glance. Simply heaven sent for our tour. A superb Ann, and not at all impossible as Raina— quite the contrary. I have told V.D. to secure her at once. Cannot understand why you did not send her to me before; she is the best discovery since Lillah. Like Dorothy Tennant rather. V.D. will settle with her unless you wire to stop him.

G.B.S.

10 Adelphi Terace, W.C.
21st June 1908.

I supplied V. D. with the necessary arguments for demanding a share of the C.L. salaries and fees from Harrison; but it really doesnt matter how they settle it, as V.D. cannot force Harrison's hand. His only weapon is a demand that the program shall be carried out as arranged with you: and, as Harrison and Watson very well know, this would hit V. & B. themselves just as hard as it would hit Harrison. I left it at this: that if the salaries were paid, and the Lantern done three times more, and Harrison convinced that if he put out the lantern he should stand in to cover £62:10:—to Housman +£12:10:—to Moorant (your wire mentioning £70. and the orchestra came too late), we could clear out at the end of the coming week, leaving Harrison to go on with G.M. at his own risk if he liked. I presume V.D. will arrange to get a percentage for the firm—in fact my consent will be conditional on that—but V.D. has not told me the terms yet—probably hasnt settled them.

The drink question has been very troublesome this past week. One disastrous matinee was followed by a brilliant evening performance. Next night Auriol had to play *both* parts. Next day, hopeless intoxication until evening; then another brilliant performance. Now Sidney Fairbrother is ready to go on on condition that if she plays once she plays ever after. Very exhausting all this. Auriol got through pluckily, but was quite impossible. I dont agree that Frances Dillon is out of the question as Raina; but there can be no question of her as Louka; so Auriol can play Raina, which consoles her for not getting Ann. She will not be as good in it as in Louka, nor, as far as I can guess without having seen F.D. act, as good as F.D. would be: but we cannot load up the tour with three leading ladies. I could not get at Nora Greenlaw to verify the sick mother plea; and V.D. jumped in and suggested Helen Rous, who will do a very good sort of Mrs. Whitefield, probably.

G.B.S.

Ayot St. Lawrence, Welwyn, Herts.
28th June 1908.

No use bothing about the Lantern. I have made up my mind about it, and nothing that a £13 house at a dogday matinee could do would change my opinion. It has just as good a chance as Prunella.

I parted with £300. yesterday to save the situation on treasury day. V.D. is to bombard me with a balance sheet presently. Harrison, he says is stony, but why should he not be, as he must know that I can pull V.D. through? However, our face has been handsomely saved to the public. Three new plays in six weeks is a sufficient sign of continued vitality.

The new dramatic committee of the Society of Authors meets tomorrow. Pinero, Sutro and Paull say they dont think they can join in view of their position on the new body; but they want to be present; and they *shall*, by George! I have prepared a special report to be issued by the new Committee, which will make the recessionists feel like worms. It concludes with a referendum asking our dramatic members will they stick or recede. This job, and having to rehearse Arms and You N.C.T. for Trevor Lowe, has rushed me to extremity. The little company isnt so bad—much better than the Savoy—relatively.

G.B.S.

The next letter marks the end of Vedrenne-Barker in London. Shaw is discussing the tours already started. Frederick Whelen,

125

who had been responsible for forming the Stage Society, was now engaged in getting the After Noon Theatre organized at His Majesty's Theatre, with H. Beerbohm Tree's co-operation, thus carrying on the Vedrenne-Barker tradition. Shaw welcomed the idea as a means of continuing the work with no responsibility for it himself. The trouble at the Authors' Society had been going on for some time, Shaw wanting the society to act as a dramatists' trade union, with objections from Pinero, Sutro and others. The meeting mentioned at the end about the National Theatre scheme followed a public demonstration that had taken place the previous May at the Lyceum theatre.

10 Adephi Terrace, W.C.

1st July 1908.

I have just forked out another £450. to Vedrenne making my total advances for the Haymarket season £1000. Add to this your £300; and mix the two with the cheering fact that this still leaves £482: 1: 2 to be provided to start the tour; that is, £1800 all told. I enclose you Vedrenne's list of liabilities. The ones ticked in red chalk are the ones which had to be met instantly. They amount to £380:14: 7. I drew the cheque for £450, partly to make the even thousand, and partly because Vedrenne wanted a margin to make advances to the less thrifty members of the Company and to Miss Dillon for her Superman dress. I leave the situation to speak for itself: you can judge my feelings by your own.

I have just telephoned Stella; she tells me that her mother has arranged a tour and that her parts are cast and that it is all over, I have told her to go upstairs and read the part of Raina, and think of all the disagreeable things that have happened between her and her mother for the last five years, and telephone me again if she thought better of it. I tried to get Mrs. Pat herself; but she is ill and not telephonable. I also tried to get Forbes to find out whether the part vacated by Lillah was still available for Auriol: but he was out. So on the whole it does not look as if we could readjust the casting, though of course the Dillon-Auriol combination is a perfectly ghastly one in point of contrast and balance.

Have you heard from Whelen about his scheme? Tree is willing to let him have His Majesty's with all its scenery, properties and staff on Tuesdays, Thursdays, and Fridays for three years, in return for a share of the profits (God help him) and first call on the plays. It does not seem to have occurred to Tree that he will occasionally want his theatre for rehearsals of his own plays; but Whelen disposes of this by saying with the frankest and most reasonable air, "No doubt there will be all sorts of difficulties." You are to be the stage manager if you will. There is to be a syndicate: this is to say, Whelen says that Lord Howard de Walden might give him £2500 and that there must be lots of other people equally unfit to be trusted with their own money. I imparted this scheme to Vedrenne yesterday. He immediately saw that it had great points as a syndicate for the purchase of the Vedrenne-Barker scenery and properties. I pointed out that the scenery would not be large enough for His Majesty's: but he said you can jack up a proscenium, and that Tree had played A Woman of No Importance with eighteen foot scenery. He also saw his chance of getting rid of Vedrenne and Barker as A Chinese Lantern producing concern, of which his soul is now weary.

This last point is the important one for us. I am at present, like V.D., fed up with the unremunerative experimental matinee drama. I have no doubt that it was good policy to keep the game alive even to the extent of loading up Getting Married with Masefield and Housman in addition to its own natural staggers; but I could not keep that game going unless I were really a rich man, which of course I am not. If Whelen's enterprise comes off it will provide for all the work that the Vedrenne-Barker matinees have been doing for the last four years. Whelen has been considerate enough not to put any of my plays on his list, which consists largely of the successes (save the mark!) of the Stage Society. This will set me free to look out for a chance of exploiting my own plays at somebody else's expense so as to re-place some of my submerged capital.

Loraine came to see me yesterday, boiling to take a theatre and begin a season of Shaw plays. The alternative for him was to accept the Wyndham part in Jones' new comedy which Harrison is going to produce at the Haymarket. Of course I flew at him in my most over-bearingly cordial manner and made him accept the Jones part on the spot, as it is a heaven-sent opportunity for him to secure the successorship to Wyndham as a second string to the bow of Ulysses. If after that he still hankers after a Shavian theatre (the enormous success in America is still sweet in his mouth), why, then we shall see. He declares that there is not the slightest difficulty in getting heaps of money. I, with the ink still wet on my pen from signing Vedrenne's cheque, receive this statement with grim geniality.

At the first meeting of the new Dramatic Sub-Committee of the Authors' Society there was no news from Barrie. Paull refused to serve. Somebody else whom I forget did the same. Pinero and Sutro asked to be allowed to attend the Committee reserving their decisions as to joining. They came, and we duly invited them to be present as guests. Jones was in the chair. As neither Jones, Sutro, nor Pinero has the slightest notion of committee procedure, we were presently in the thick of a frightful squabble. Sutro said that the appointment of the Sub-Committee was a gross attack on the new body; that our conduct in attempting to kidnap its prominent members was a disgraceful trick; and that he could not possibly consent to be present. This went on for about half an hour, when Sutro shook the dust off his feet and went. Pinero, not knowing what to do, thought it would be safer to follow Sutro's example. Comyns Carr remained, but explained that in principle he was absent. I then moved a report which I had concocted, which is to be sent to all our dramatic members, asking them to say whether they desire to remain with the old Society or to secede. It can also be sent to the Secretary of the new body with an offer of sufficient copies to send round to all his people who are not also our people. It piles up an imposing display of the work we have been doing for the dramatic profession in the past, and it gives a staggering demonstration of the ludicrous inadequacy of the resources of the Secession, and the absolute necessity of combining the financial resources of the whole body of Authors for the common defence. Its effect was crushing. We meet again tomorrow to consider it further.

Hare, Pinero, Lord Lytton and myself met Lord Esher and Lord Plymouth at the house of the latter yesterday to pick the committee for the National Theatre scheme. There is no slackening of energy in that business.

That is all the news for the present—all I can remember in this rush to get away, at all events.

G.B.S.

The "money" referred to below was what Shaw had lost on the Haymarket season. The Rev. Harold Davidson, who had been an actor before ordination, was afterwards ejected from his living at Stiffkey and became notorious as "the clergyman in a barrel." Barker's salary was in respect of the tour. The Shaws were just off for a Continental holiday.

10, Adelphi Terrace, W.C.
4th July 1908.

Do not bother about the money. No doubt I shall have to find it. Let us hope the tour will bring it back.

I strongly advised Lillah to go to the Empire. The other day at the Authors' Society Committee somebody sniffed at writing for the music halls; and Pinero and myself with a common impulse, exclaimed "Why not"? I have serious thoughts myself of taking to the half-hour play.

A clergyman named Harold Davidson, formerly an actor, now being bored to death in a living at Stiffkey in Norfolk to which the Marquis of Lansdowne presented him, declares that he has got a substantial capital with which to adapt a certain building in London to the purposes of a new and glorified Stage Society which is to give performances every night at its own theatre. He says Lady de Grey is interested &c., &c., and is of course looking up to Lord Howard de Walden.

Vedrenne consulted me on the subject of your salary—suggested £15; with say, £10 extra if you were unscrupulous enough to ask for it. I said that I thought you would probably expect at least £35. I said you can get £40. from the Stage Society if you dun Thompson for it.

Your letter was duly read at the Dramatic Sub-Committee of the Society of Authors. As usual, a series of insults to Thring. Comyns Carr is not on the Theatre Sub-Committee of the National scheme: Lytton chucked him off without mercy. What he will say when he finds out, heaven only knows.

I am afraid the rectory at Ayot will be uninhabitable in

August. The workmen will be doing up the house and setting the drains right. Higgs will be learning to drive a motor, and the rest of the staff will be scattered about holidaying.

I was weak enough in my hurry to return a comparatively soft answer to Mrs. Pat. Result, she returns to the charge in her most governessy mood, calling me names, and preaching about good manners, good breeding, good taste, etc., etc., etc., etc., etc., etc. I have replied most unchivalrously; and expect poor Stella will have a bad day of it; but she will find it easier to get loose next time. Auriol Lee flatly refused to give up the tour on any terms, London engagement or no London engagement.

I start in a few minutes. Goodbye.

G.B.S.

They went first to Sweden and Shaw wrote on a picture post-card containing a portrait of Auguste Strindberg:

Stockholm.

This great man reached the summit of his career when he met the immortal G.B.S. at the Theatre Interne at Stockholm on the 16th. July 1908 at one o/clock in the afternoon. At 1.25, he said in German, "At two o/clock I am going to be sick." On this strong hint the party broke up.

When Shaw was offered the Nobel Prize for literature in 1925 he donated it to the Anglo-Swedish Literary Alliance, one of the first actions of which was to publish in English an edition of Strindberg's plays.

Even on holiday Shaw does not neglect business and writes about John Bull's Other Island *and the other plays to be done on the Vedrenne-Barker tour in Dublin.*

On the Baltic en route for Lubeck.
19th July 1908.

Stockholm has long since disappeared beneath the horizon. The fact to grasp firmly is that the tour goes to Dublin, where Hearn has already made a success as Matt Haffigan. This means that

Dublin will stand Hearn as an Irishman. But it wont stand Sherbrooke as one. Furthermore, Hearn is a bad Ramsden and a good last-actor. There is no reason whatever why Ramsden should not be Sheeny; and he will be enormously comic if Sherbrooke plays him. The moral is obvious: Hearn as Malone—Nicola, Sherbrooke as Ramsden and Petkoff.

They reached Lübeck on the 21st July, and Charlotte sent Barker a card from Hamburg to say they were off to Bayreuth the next day by car.

Hotel Vier Jahreszeiten, Munchen.
(Post marked Aug. 8 '08)
I have just seen Candida and How He Lied at the Residency Theatre. I shall never be the same man again. They dropped the curtain for ten seconds each time and got through in 90 minutes. The Eugene was a perfect H. G. Wells hero, only needing a terrier, a straw hat, a bicycle agency, and a copy of the Sporting Times to make him complete. He was a bit of an athlete, and jumped in the chair with his legs crossed very well. In How He Lied he sat on the piano keyboard and Teddy banged the bass with him. Burgess and Candida were good; but the performance, on the whole was a horror. As I see Don Giovanni announced for Saturday I shall wait for it.

G.B.S.

Shaw draws Barker's attention to Schnitzler's sequence of dialogues, which Barker afterwards paraphrased under the title Anatol.

Munchen.
11th August 1908.
Do not plank Hankin's American reputation on The Return of the Prodigal: it is not fat enough. Try either Cassilis or The Last of the de Mullins. This is really important. I dont know either The Awakening or The Eldest Son. I saw Anatole last night. Tristan today: Caesar tomorrow (Sunday), after which I will write

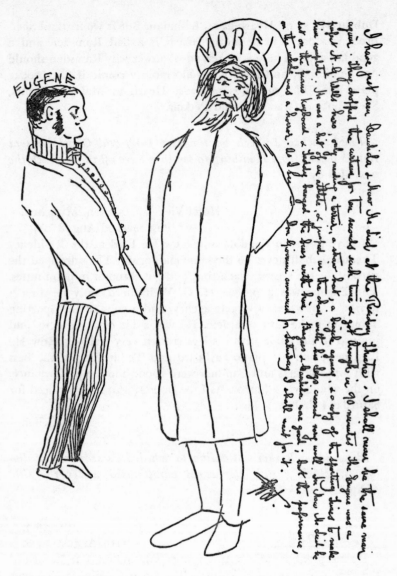

"The performance on the whole was a horror."

again. Shubert should be offered power, if any of the plays catches powerfully on, to take another theatre and run it. Otherwise he will kill the rest of the repertory for it. Anatole was very like Daly. The Farewell Supper was immense—a triumph of abandonment for the lady.

G.B.S.

The following was written on six picture-postcards.

Nördlingen. August 11. 1908.

(1)

On Friday I shall be at the Schloss Hotel, Heidelberg: at least I have sent on the heavy luggage thither. I write this in a delightful medieval walled town called Nördlingen on my way from Munich to Rothenburg. At Donauworth we struck some lovely country; and I began to revive a little. I have given up the notion of coming back to London for the Authors' Society meeting on the 20th, as Charlotte does not want to be left for a week between the Continent and her engaged rooms in Mallaranny on the west coast of

(2)

Ireland. We shall wander about with our car between this and Bremen, where we shall take a Nord-Deutschen Lloyd liner for Southampton arriving in time to reach Ireland at the beginning of September. Meanwhile, communication will be precarious if not impossible. I want a holiday very badly. I used to want change: now I want rest, especially as the worries of travelling used to be a complete change from the high and strenuous activities of my prime, whereas now the vulgar worries of business are just

(3)

like the travelling worries; and the only sign of improvement in my condition is that whereas I was crushed I am now exasperated. Another day in Munich would have driven me mad: the day after tomorrow I shall feel that another day's motoring will murder me. The Mozart performances were very interesting. The electric turntable would be capital but for the indelicacy of working it in sight of the audience to shew it off. How they manage to change the sets without making a noise I cannot imagine. Figaros Hochzert

133

was delightful, Don Giovanni (see Matthews as the Don) a
hideous disappointment, Cosi fan tutte the most interesting of all
to me, as I had never heard it before. Mottl can conduct Mozart.
He is better than the ordinary Covent Garden nincompoop, because he is vigorous, and respects the music, making it at least
sound masterly and powerful; but he does not understand the
Mozart andante, with its peculiar tenderness and delicacy; and he
conducted the window trios in the second act of the Don as if it
were a coarse joke. Cosi

(5)

fan tutte is very remarkable. I really think I'd rather have
composed it than the Don. As to the rehearsals, you will fail as
Bluntschli if you set Hamer to act Sergius as you did. You really
killed Loraine by not giving him the necessary contrast. Tell him
(Hamer) to act Sergius as if he were acting Hamlet, but let him
alone: he doesnt do it half badly except in bits where he is too
young to do it at all. If you try to prevent him from acting,
you will make him impossible—paralyse him and get nothing.
Let him read

(6)

Byron,—Sara—the Cosair &c &c—and play and feel like that,
leaving the irony to come from the words—Mrs. Wheeler will
never be any good in Widowers' Houses; but the practice and the
starring may easily develop her into quite a striking stage figure
for certain parts. When she is worked into all the richness that
she has hitherto been unable to develop for want of opportunity
and nursing she may quite possibly be the person you want for
the mother in your new play; at all events you might let her begin
on a number two tour of it.

G.B.S.

*On the road from Dinkelsbühl to Rothenburg they had a slight
accident as Shaw relates on the following card.*

Rothenburg 12 August 1908.
The motor having backjumped & sent Charlotte like a rocket

to the roof of the car (a limousine, unluckily) she is now uncertain whether her neck is broken or not. She leans to the belief that it is. Anyhow we shall stay here tomorrow to give her a rest.

G.B.S.

Langenburg.

August. 1908.

On the road again. We were stuck for four days in Rothenburg, Charlotte having fever and a bad throat after the Bayreuth sani-tation. All right now. There is a hydro in the valley below Rothenburg—an ideal place to write plays in for victims of cir-cumstances like you and Harry Arthur Jones.

G.B.S.

There follows one of two picture-postcards of which the first has been lost on the subject of the relations between Vedrenne and Barker, which were by no means good.

Heidelberg.

19th August 1908.

. . . all your earnings and he all his; and both draw equal shares. Thus all his Waller and West End manager's takings would go in; and so would all your tantiennes and royalties. This will bring home to him the fact that he is drawing money in at least three capacities out of his 24 hours a day just as you will be drawing it in two capacities, and the fact that you draw nominally from V. & B. whilst he draws from Waller and the W.E.M. doesn't alter the economic aspect at all. If all your time belongs to V. & B. then so does all his: if there is to be a pool, everything must go in, if not more reason for him to share your salary as an actor than for you to share his as manager and secretary. No use not explaining this to him: he will see it at once when it is put in this way; and he had better yield to reason than to force me to feel sore about it.

G.B.S.

Shaw is still advising Barker about his personal arrangements with the partnership over the tour. Shaw's dislike for travelling, which interfered so much with his work, is again expressed.

Heidelberg.
19th August 1908.

I have your letter, and one from Vedrenne. I have sent a reply addressed to the firm at Shaftesbury Avenue, dealing with the question of salary, profit sharing, &c. I propose therein £20+£30=£50 a week for partner's salary and actor's salary. The acting is quite a separate thing; and if it is kept so there will be no question of inequality. Do not hesitate to send business letters. I am fed up with vagabondage, and with the cat and dog life I lead with poor Charlotte, who takes every unguarded expression of my loathing of travelling as a personal insult to herself. Another month of it would end in a divorce. I held out fairly well until Munich; but 3 weeks is my limit: since then I have been very bad company for myself and worse for her. Dont allude to this in correspondence: it is not safe until we are back again at our ain fireside.

G.B.S.

[*To Mrs. Granville Barker*]

Arnsberg.
24th August 1908.

I got your letter at Marburg. Somehow I have never yet succeeded in achieving a sketch; and I dont think I could make it a success without a lot of scenic machinery; but I shall turn it over in my imagination, or rather let it turn over and see what will come of it.

G.B.S.

Arnsberg.
25th August 1908.

When you say you have corrected Ann Leete and Voysey for the press, I hope you dont imply that you are going to publish them without Waste. That would be a fatal mistake—just the sort of hopeless monstrous error that would appeal to a publisher. Get Waste ready as fast as you can: the three plays must be published in one volume, with preface and portrait, before next spring.

G.B.S.

Darmstadt. 1908.

A pleasing novelty in this exhibition is a model cemetery with Art Nouveau tombstones.

Also evidence in the picture gallery that Teddy Craig has founded a school in Germany.

G.B.S.

They visited the ancient and handsome town of Münster on their return, and from there stopped on the way at Gütersloh, which provoked from Shaw the following outburst:

Gütersloh. 27 August 1908.

Thus far into the bowels, etc., etc. We are stopping for lunch— and Heavenly Life Force, WHAT a lunch! *Sweet* omelette (fines herbes, indeed!) and crab apples—on the way from Münster to Detmold. Münster was rather a success. Tomorrow, excursions from Detmold. Saturday, Detmold to Onasbruck; Sunday, Onasbruck to Bremen; thence to London all, & less such days as this to us befall.

G.B.S.

After they came home, Shaw saw some of the plays on tour in England, and wrote to Vedrenne about a performance of Man and Superman:

15th October 1908.

I came within an inch of suicide and murder . . . Ann Whitefield looks like a dowdy Brixton widow of forty . . . I feel no further disposition to pursue the heart-breaking trade of playwright and shall henceforth devote myself to the advancement of the human race as politician and essayist.

A fortnight later, writing about another provincial performance he said:

28th October 1908.

Indignant letters from disciples in the country and a chance press cutting reveal the fact that Trevor Lowe has announced

137

Y.N.C.T. as a farcical comedy, and has cut Mrs. Clandon's speech out of the first act. Kindly obliterate Trevor Lowe from the book of life and tell him not to accept any further dates. If he wants to be a waiter in a farcical comedy, let him try Pink Dominoes.

In the middle of November when Barker was playing with the company in Dublin he fell ill with typhoid fever, which was first diagnosed by a homeopathic doctor, who did not know him, as influenza. Vedrenne got the news of Barker's illness and at once phoned to Miss McCarthy, urging her to go over, as his condition seemed serious. She was then playing in What Every Woman Knows. *She went to Dublin where she was met by Lady Gregory, and finding Barker in a desperate condition they went round the city to get another doctor to take over his case, without avail, until Lady Gregory prevailed on the Abbey Theatre doctor to do so. Barker was recovering for some time after, and Shaw's long letters to him indicate his kindness to the sick man, giving him as much news as possible of what was going on in London, particularly about the William Poel production of Gilbert Murray's version of* The Bacchae *at the Court Theatre on 10 November, the National Theatre Committee, and the troubles of the Fabians.*

Ayot St. Lawrence, Welwyn, Herts.
15th November 1908.

My dear Barker,

Taylor Platt came to Liverpool yesterday (Saturday) to tell me that he had left you at 104°. Irish temperature is fortunately 2° higher than English; but still even 102° is pretty warm. Let us know when you get down to normal; for Charlotte would certainly have gone over to nurse you yesterday but for the fact that she was herself in bed in much the same plight: I sent your telegram on to Wheeler; but I now learn that it will not reach him until this evening. Therefore you will hear from him a day later than I had counted on. Liverpool also threw me back a day: I delivered a noble address there and ended with a soul-stirring appeal for a municipal theatre.

The Bacchae was, on the whole, good business for Lillah: it brought out the sort of thing she can do that nobody else can do;

and the mesmeric scene came off immensely. But of course the performance was an absurdity all the same. The four women yowled inhumanly. They remembered my precepts fairly well in the first chorus; but they soon got hysterical; and if some property on the lines of the Wooden Horse of Troy, but shaped like a tom cat had come forth, fascinated by their wailings, the effect would have been superb. As it was, nothing better was to be expected than Max's article in the Saturday. The gay chorus leader sang prettily and spoke clearly; but she was not classical; and some of her music would have revolted the Girls of Gothenburg. And then the curtains were a horrible mistake. Greek plays require the open air: and Duchess of Malfi effects are no use in them. Lillah's entrance was most trying. She had to step out from behind a dark curtain into a crude blaze of light which was all wrong for her open air costume, and produced a haggard, raw, eyeball-insulting effect. I have persuaded her to be discovered next time in a robe-cloak, with her back to the audience, and to turn on them for her opening lines instead of entering. On Friday morning I went through the part with her, and acted the first scene with Pentheus with such superb realism that she got uncomfortable and finally stopped and said "It's no use: I cant act with you; you make me feel that you dont believe in me a bit." I never even told her that the sceptic was Pentheus, not G.B.S. because I wanted to get on to the later scenes.

Some of the cuts are very stupid. Poel doesnt understand Lillah technically, and doesnt understand Dionyseus temperamentally. He pulls off the big bits, and gets the story across the footlights; but he throws away a good deal too, and does not quite realize how very bad is the best that his choreoguses can do.

The National Theatre is being organized apace. Esher and I have imposed a sound democratic constitution on it: the director must carry a Standing Committee of seven with him; and I have imposed the yoke of the treasurer heavily on him. The staff is to be Director, Treasurer, and Man of Letters: three *not* in one, nor one in three. Pinero had a fancy for allowing the Director one play of his own choice, whether his mother would let him or no (so to speak); but on closer consideration we all saw that it would not do. As Esher and I are the oldest hands at public committee work, we get our own way pretty well. We have now finished our statutes (or think we have) and are about to start on the bye-laws. Meanwhile, we are agreed that we must get £100,000 in the hat before it goes round, or we shall get £5 notes from people who ought to give us a thousand. The £100,000 is called my uncle's banknote. Said uncle was a clergyman. When he preached a charity sermon, he always put a bank note in the plate before the churchwarden started with it. He replaced it in his pocket subsequently. I told this to the committee: hence the phrase above quoted.

Esher thinks we may get a Knighthood for Pinero next June. He approves warmly.

I saw Forbes-Robertson in the Jerome play on Thursday. It was quite as good as I thought it when I read it. The third act is the weak spot; but the first and second would carry a worse one through.

Hankin, bedridden in Brompton Square, writes endless letters to everybody, and talks of an operation. What is the matter with him? It is time for him to get to work at De Mullin if he means to assist in the production.

The Fabian Basis meetings are developing into a series of personal attacks on one another by the leaders of the Society. Headlam's paper was an attack on "the bureaucratic Collectivist" (Webb); and Pease's paper was an attack on me as an absurd imposter in economics. I up and said "Who will be Mr. Hobson's victim"? (Roars). The women asked urgency for a resolution calling on the Home Secretary to put Mrs. Pank and Christabel in the first division. The Nursery protested because they had not been allowed to move the Grayson resolution last time. Hobson said he would allow the resolution to be put provided it passed without discussion. "Is there any opposition"? said he. "Yes," shrieked the Nursery. "I appeal to you," said Hobson. "Is there any opposition?" The Nursery—molto crescendo—"Yes." Hobson looked pained. "For the third time, is there any opposition?" he repeated. The Nursery—con tutta la forza—"Y E S." "Then I declare the resolution carried," said Hobson. Struck dumb by this coup, and intimidated by the triumphant cheers of the Feminists, the Nursery subsided until after Pease's lecture, when

Blanco White moved that Hobson leave the chair. Sidney Herbert seconded; and Hobson put it to the meeting. FOR 2. AGAINST, all the rest. Applause and curtain.

I am summoned away and must break off.

G.B.S.

Dr. C. E. Wheeler, mentioned in the previous letter, a distinguished homoeopathic physician, was the chairman of the council of management of the Stage Society and a great friend of Barker's. The National Theatre Committee was getting on its long way, Viscount Esher was the father of the present Lord Esher. A. W. Pinero got his knighthood. J. Forbes-Robertson was playing in The Passing of the Third Floor Back *at the St. James's Theatre, one of the greatest successes of his career. St. John Hankin's comedy* The Last of the De Mullins *was performed by the Stage Society on 10 December. The Fabian Society was passing through one of its most tempestuous periods. The Fabian S. G. Hobson was the originator of the Guild Socialist movement. He afterwards resigned from the Society. The Fabian Nursery was a section of the society intended for those who were young in socialism.*

St. John Hankin's play is referred to again in the following letter. It was his last, except for two one-act pieces, for Hankin died less than two years later at the age of thirty-nine. It was his most ambitious effort. He described it as "a play without a preface." The leading part was played by Lillah McCarthy, and Shaw gives an entertaining account of the Stage Society's production. His recurrent headaches, and Charlotte Shaw's fondness for Barker are also mentioned.

The National Theatre Committee was engaged in defining how the proposed theatre should be administered and who should direct it; there was to be an appeal for £500,000, but this and other matters had first to be settled. The Archer-Barker scheme, called the "Blue Book," was by no means favoured, and, to cut a long story short, Shaw's account of the committee is evidence of the ineptitude that characterized its conduct.

Shaw returns to the affairs of another committee, that of the dramatic sub-committee of the Society of Authors. We see how

he loved committee work, at which he was in fact very good,
much too good for the average committee man, who is either
merely awkward, or pursuing an interest of his own to the exclu-
sion of everything else, or, as the majority is, simply acquiescent.
He is cheering up the convalescent Barker, still in Dublin.

10 Adelphi Terrace, W.C.
7th December 1908.

My dear Barker,

I came up to London yesterday (Sunday) to see the first of The
Last of the De Mullins. Lillah was all right: the play being on
her shoulders, she rose nobly to the occasion as Mrs. Crummles
and displayed great professional competence, and steadiness in
addition to her own special fascination. But the production was
not good enough. The scene between Janet and her young man
in the second act is exquisitely written—the best thing Hankin
has yet done; but it requires consummate handling, and a hero
who, though an ex-bicyclist, is emphatically not a common-place
type, with a stick and a pipe, and a half-bred black and tan.
Unfortunately, Vernon Steel took the greatest possible care to
be just this common-place kind of bicyclist. Although the bicycling episode had taken place nine years previously, he still wore
his bicycling costume, and as he climbed over the stile he sucked
at an enormous briar pipe in a manner that proclaimed that his
name was Dick and that he was the vulgar sentimental hero of a
thousand bad plays. In any case, the skill and finish required by
the scene were far beyond him: and its delicacy and beauty were
consequently obliterated. Also, the mother (Adela Measor) though
very good in the 1st Act, entirely failed to keep the 2nd Act in
character, and simply turned on her stock sympathetic pathos
with the effect of turning poor Lillah into a heartless daughter
trampling on the noblest instincts of melodramatic motherhood.
The young man's fiancee was very rotten indeed. It was not her
fault; it was simply a miscast. In the 3rd Act Lillah appealed
with extraordinary gusto to every unmarried woman of twenty-
eight in the house to go straight out and procure a baby at once
without the slightest regard to law or convention. As Lillah regards this a most obvious and reasonable doctrine, she had no

idea of the effect she was producing in the audience. At the end of the Act the majority were simply afraid to applaud: the thing had gone quite beyond mere play-acting for them, and although they were interested, they felt—quite rightly—that to clap such sentiments would be to vote for them. Consequently, though there were curtain calls, they were forced by a partly friendly, partly assenting minority. Anything like a hit in the ordinary uproarious way was quite out of the question. The play will have to fight its way like A Doll's House.

I saw Lillah this morning. She had not slept well, and looked as if she had been boiled and wrung out but not yet mangled and ironed; but she is all right, and agrees that there is no need for her to go over and convey you back. We have neglected her scandalously during your troubles.

I had to go to Edinburgh on the 25th, which involved two successive nights in sleeping cars. This was followed by a champion headache which left me in a condition in which Lillah and you and the whole universe might have perished in the most frightful torments without causing me any sensation except one of malicious satisfaction. Charlotte sent for Wheeler, who prescribed pulsatilla. Charlotte's medical curiosity being aroused by this, she looked up her handbook of homoeopathy to find what pulsatilla was good for. She found it was good for milk troubles. It was rather lucky, by the way, that Charlotte got ill at the same time as you did. She developed a high temperature, which did not particularly inconvenience me, and a perfectly appalling temper, which did. But for this, she would certainly have gone over; stood 14 Herbert Place on its head; and most likely killed you. She returned to reason and to health simultaneously; so you were spared.

It may interest you to know that the average return from the beginning of the tour to the departure from Dublin was £62:1:7$\frac{44}{79}$.

Your illness is rather a godsend from the point of view of the progress of the National Theatre. You would have simply howled if you had attended the Committee and seen your beautiful plot for getting half a million to play with in a theatre of your own scattered to the winds by the breath of democracy. The one thing that the Director must make up his mind to is that he must not only be able to manage a theatre but also a committee. Of course every manager will say, as you do (*vous êtes orfevre, M. Josselin*), that the proper thing is for the Board to meet twice a year and receive his report. That is what every vestry clerk says about his Council. All the same, the vestry clerk has to square a vestry meeting every fortnight: and the manager of the National Theatre will have to do the same. It would be impossible to go to the country and ask them for half a million of money, not to give the nation a theatre, but to give some private and perfectly irresponsible person a theatre. It is good enough for the King to have to act by the advice of his ministers, and for even the Kaiser to have his speeches handed to him in writing by Von Bulow, it is good enough for the manager of the National Theatre to have to do what every manager of joint stock enterprises has to do. After all, he will be more independent than a Trade Union secretary; and as a trade union secretary is the most absolute autocrat, Redford perhaps excepted, in the country, the real danger is that the Director will have too much power instead of too little. Anyhow, neither Esher nor any other man experienced in public affairs will hear of the scheme in the Archer-Barker book, as it is quite openly planned to make the Director supreme. There is only one condition on which you can establish an autocracy, and that is, by providing such a minute and elaborate constitution and Articles of War that the Director, like the Captain of a battleship, has no more freedom than his subordinates. If you want elasticity and humanity—in other words, if you want Art—you must have democracy.

The Constitution we are elaborating is a wildly illogical affair, but what it will come to is a standing committee of rather helpless inexperts, who will be face to face with a staff of three experts. Expert number one will be the Director. Expert number two, who in his own department will be as a steel curb in the mouth of the Director, will be the Treasurer, who will have nothing to do with the artistic business of the theatre, but, like Hector Thompson in the Stage Society, will force the Director to keep his productions within the estimates. I have insisted strongly on this in view of the possibility of your becoming the

Director. Expert number three, not necessarily an important person, though an able man in the berth can make himself so, will be the Reader of Plays. These three will attend the committee meetings and make their reports. It will be the business of the Director to procure the support of his two colleagues and the assent of the Committee to his plans. If he cannot do that, which is a comparatively simple job, he cannot manage a theatre in the way in which a National Theatre should be managed. The Irving way of being "Governor," and simply ordering about a gang of employees whilst a bribed retinue blew property trumpets, is impracticable for us. The Director will have no funds to bribe anyone with; and as he will be forbidden to act in the theatre himself, he will be unable to retrieve, by a personal success, the depression set up by a company of worms.

The blue book is all very well; but it has been superseded by those pages from the book of life which we turned over at the Court Theatre. I myself am steering carefully clear of it until I have given effect to the ideas I have got from actual experience. It has two weaknesses in its foundation. In the first place, it madly exaggerates the probable takings. It has been really mischievous in this way, because I had some difficulty in persuading the Committee that they ought not to rely on a higher average than £75. a night. You and I know that this is a sporting estimate: but the Committee, under the influence of the estimate of the book, were inclined to regard it as a staggering come-down.

In the second place, the selection of plays is obsolete. Archer's notion was that as the programs were merely hypothetical, the selection of plays did not matter and might just as well have consisted altogether of fictitious pieces. It would have been all right if the list had been fictitious. But by naming so many actual plays, you created an atmosphere which was quite the wrong atmosphere, and suggested wrong lines of speculation as to the future. The consequence is that at the Committee meetings, whenever a hypothetical play had to be put forward in argument, we began by citing a fictitious play imagined by Archer. So after playing wtih this unconvincing ghost for a whole, an irresistible tendency set in to begin every argument with the words "Suppose, for instance, we were to produce a piece by Mr. Bernard Shaw."

This got at, first Pinero's sense of humor, and then the rest of the Committee's, with the result that it is now a standing joke always to suppose a play by me, more especially when some particularly disastrous consequences have to be anticipated. No doubt this is very good fun. But it prevents the Committee from realizing that there are other talents available. You should have put into those lists every name that shewed the slightest promise.

One of the points which bothers me is how to reconcile the necessary neutrality in the directorship with the genius necessary to make a great success of the theatre. In discussing the possibility of getting a good standing committee, we have been repeatedly reduced to console ourselves with assuring one another that we ourselves should make an excellent committee; but thereupon has arisen the point that as the members of the committee should be disinterested, they had better not be actors or authors; and I suppose the article which forbids the Director to cast himself for a part in the theatre, would also make it rather difficult to allow him to present one of his own pieces for production. This cuts out Pinero, myself, yourself, Tree, Comyns Carr, etc., etc., etc., It looks to me as if we should have to put up with such direct interference as we can effect as producers of our own plays, and bring our general criticism to play on the scheme by communications from the Society of Authors.

This brings me to the other business. The last event in that campaign was a conference of the Dramatic Sub-Committee of the Society of Authors with Pinero, Raleigh and Barrie as ambassadors from the new organization. To them we made the following handsome offer. The members of the Dramatic Sub-Committee are all to resign, thereby creating 12 vacancies for the managing Committee of the S. of A. to fill. Pinero is to call a meeting of dramatic authors all and sundry, attached and unattached. This meeting is to elect 12 persons, and to declare that it would consider the profession satisfactorily represented by a committee consisting of these apostles. This being done, it will be up to the Society of Authors to fill the 12 vacancies on its Dramatic Sub-Committee by the 12 apostles. If it does so, then all outsiders are to join the Society, and we are to live happily ever after. This sounds simple: and as the new body is not only in the minority, but is evidently feeble, half-hearted, bewildered by the staggering activity of the Society of Authors, and overwhelmed by its eye-opening reports and drafts, I daresay the matter will go through on the lines suggested. The difficulty is that the Dramatic Sub-Committee happens to be a very good one—so much so that there are, at the very outside, only four seats on it which can be handed over to the other side without lowering the quality of the Committee. Therefore, unless we are to do considerable mischief, at least eight of the present Sub-Committee must be re-elected. On that there may be a row; but we must take our chance of it.

Yours ever,
G. Bernard Shaw.

H. Granville Barker, Esq.
14, Herbert Place,
Dublin.

3

The Censorship, the National
Theatre, et Cetera

Here we have letters that touch upon a variety of matters, all of importance in the development of the friendship between Shaw and Barker. They cover the year 1909, a year of importance in theatrical history. Granville Barker had returned home and he and Lillah had gone to the H. G. Wells' at Sandgate for Christmas. The first reference is to the National Theatre Committee, of which much has already been said in earlier letters. Frederick Whelen's After Noon Theatre at His Majesty's did not last the intended three years; it finished in December 1909. The reference to Charles Frohman is the first indication that this manager was interested in the higher drama. He was responsible for putting on Galsworthy's Strife *the following March, and eleven months later he started the repertory. Tono Bungay is, of course, H. G. Wells.*

Ayot St. Lawrence, Welwyn, Herts.
31st Dec. 1908.

Charlotte is in Shropshire. I am here in Ayot St. Lawrence, snowed up and slushed up in the filthiest manner. I shall have to get up to town tomorrow somehow to attend the committee. I shouldnt come if I were you: you cant get any grip at this eleventh hour, and I daresay the prelude will pass with all suggestions of the confounded poor man cut out. We should get £5 notes instead of thousands if we began in that key. First get your theatre out of the rich: then capture it for the million if you like—though *I* want it for about a dozen righteous men.

The afternoon theatre has had to fall back on Bashville for the 26th. Such is the end of the first attempt at a Shawless theatre.

148

Letter just to hand from Lillah about Frohman. It shall be attended to.

The car is here—at least the steel part of it. The splashboards &c are mostly lying about in the lanes. Charlotte wrecked it the first day. The professional kept her in countenance by knocking off the paddle box against the gate. Higgs & I took up the game then. No room left to insult old Tono Bungay; but you may give my love to Jane.

G.B.S.

The following note has to do with the National Theatre Committee:

Ayot St. Lawrence, Welwyn, Herts.
1st Jan. 1909.

Esher raised the technical point that the preamble was outside our reference, and should be submitted to the whole executive. He was right, of course, though we could have got round that if we had wanted. However, we didnt. There was a long talk and a letter from Tree &c. &c; and you will have to let them talk themselves out at several meetings before they can ascertain either what they mean or what the preamble means. I jollified Phil considerably over his speech.

I start for Edstaston in the car tomorrow.

G.B.S.

John Galsworthy's drama about industrial conflict, Strife, *was performed at matinees at Frohman's theatre, The Duke of York's, starting on 9 March, the date of the following letter. It was produced by Barker, the leading part, John Anthony, being taken with great success by Norman McKinnel. The part of Edgar was played by C. M. Hallard: Hubert Harben was the actor preferred by Shaw for the part. Enid was Ellen O'Mally. O. P. Heggie played Harry Trench, the company secretary. Lillah McCarthy was Madge Thomas, the miner's sick wife.*

9th March 1909.

Strife was very good business for everybody. Edgar was bad: Harben would have been better; but the rest were all good fits

149

and did well. I think the attempt to hustle the dialogue between Edgar and Enid at the beginning of the 3rd Act is a mistake, better take it quietly and let them cough. Also I think the obvious suppression of poor Ellen O'M. in the first act to avoid taking the shine out of Heggie's remarkable imitation of you afterwards was a totally unjustifiable piece of tyranny; but with these exceptions the production was superb. The scene of the men's meeting is spun out both unskilfully and without knowledge of mob oratory (give me Brutus and Mark Antony) but Galsworthy earns the right to err to that extent. The play came out very solid and absorbing, and was an important event in stage history; and more one cannot demand.

Lillah as the old hand with the sure stroke impressed Tree and the experts in addition to producing a great effect poetically.

The Shaws had started on another Continental holiday, and Shaw's correspondence, as usual on such occasions, was conducted on picture postcards. In his small clear writing he could get a great deal in the space available.

We start tomorrow for Tunis, taking Biskra on our way. What with a railway strike here on lines that go only 15 miles an hour at best, and a postal strike in France, communication seems impossible. In case of emergency, Miss Gillmore, Royal Anchor Hotel, Liphook, Hants (until 1st April) has certain addresses at which telegrams MAY reach me.

G.B.S.

Bougie. 28th March 1909.

Thus far into the bowels of the land have we marched on without impediment. It really bangs everything in the way of scenery and climate. Forbes-Robertson wants me to do a sketch for the National Union of Women's Suffrage Societies or some such body. I think I shall do it to prevent myself succumbing to the fits of fury that all this frightful waste of time and money brings on—or soon will bring on. I keep them off at present by reading the Koran.

G.B.S.

Shaw did what the feminists wanted by writing the farcical satire, Press Cuttings, *which was prohibited by the censor because Prime Minister Balsquith in the play, who gave way to the women, was too easily a representation of the actual man.*

Grand Hotel, Constantine.

3/4/09.

Timgad is the place for you if you like unearthed Roman cities. The theatre is still quite practicable. We drove 100 miles north from Biskra yesterday and 100 more today. Result, a dramatic change of climate. At Biskra, exquisite soft heat and southern airs: here, a cold as of liquid air evaporating on the skin; rain in colossal blobs instead of drops; and a wind against which I had to hold the car straight by main force.

G.B.S.

Le Calle, Constantine.

4th April 09.

Do you think, in view of Mansfield's success with Peer Gynt, that Frohman could be induced to add it to the list of Frohmannational Theatricalities? He could spend money on it visibly; and he knows the value of that.

G.B.S.

Shaw never gave up urging Barker to produce Ibsen's masterpiece; but he did not attempt it. The picture on the card used for the following epistle was of a Moorish musician.

Souk el Arba, Tunis.

7th April 1909.

This gentleman seems to me quite equal to the musician of Franz Hals. We have escaped from the bad weather and shall reach Tunis tomorrow. We crossed the frontier today. I have not seen an English paper since I left, and know absolutely nothing of contemporary history except that they have actually made Brieux an Academician. I now think I shall catch my boat for Southampton at Algiers on the 21st (Friday) and reappear in London the following week.

G.B.S.

151

The Frohman Repertory Theatre was on the way, and Shaw promised a new play. Harcourt's bill mentioned below related to the censorship of plays. The secret that a mere actress, Lillah McCarthy, was responsible for securing the remarkable gift to the National Theatre Committee was well kept, for even Shaw at that moment was not in it; but the Meyer contribution did not encourage other wealthy men to follow his example. His postcards describe his not always pleasant experiences; Shaw went on these travels only because Charlotte insisted that it was good to get away from people and work.

Tunis.
8th April 1909.

Found your letter here waiting for me. I gather that Strife has been transferred to the Haymarket evening bill and that Frohman has swallowed up Harrison. I will not rehearse in September for anybody: let Barrie do it. Mahomet can wait until Redford is abolished (how is Harcourt's bill getting on?) I will write for the Frohman enterprise *ad hoc.* Who gave Mrs. L. the £70,000? was it all one subscription? Nothing to prevent us starting on that tomorrow. I met a Count Gleichen, brother of Helena, on the boat. We conferred on various matters. He left at Gib. Return journey now impending.

G.B.S.

La Calle, Constantine.
14th April 1909.

Today, the 13th, we left Tunisia and are back again in Algeria, but under creepy-crawly circumstances. There is only one hotel of a possible kind here (not very possible either) ; and it was full when we arrived. We are in a frightful place: I cannot bear to go to bed. The sanitary arrangements consist mainly of the stairs. Indescribable. I really cant go on.

G.B.S.

Biskra.

I have this day ridden for two hours on a camel; and my tail is sore in consequence; but my seat on this most difficult of mounts was admitted to be superb. I have also seen, but not touched, the improper woman of the Outlet Nail, and seen a star artist disguised as a Mahometan Zealot licking red hot iron, sticking himself full of skewers; and holding a blazing branch under his vest. In short I am at Biskra, my southernest point.

G.B.S.

Hamman—Meskoutine.
18.4.09.

(1)

I find that I am in for five days more than I bargained for. There is no room in the ship that sails on the 23rd, so I must wait for the Bremen, which sails on the 28th. If you have any news that needs pondering *en* voyage, perhaps a letter by return addressed to me Passenger SS Bremen Algiers to Southampton, c/o Norddeutschen Lloyd, 3, Boulevard de la Republique, Algiers, might catch me. You can judge by the

(2)

postmarks on these cards how long a letter takes to travel, allowing for the fact that Hamman Meskoutine, where I post this, is 24 hours by rail from Algiers, and that as there is only one train a day, a letter may, by missing it, take 48 hours. Also there is some luck in the crossing from Marsailles as the boats dont go every day, and take 24 hours when they do go. This is a rum place, all boiling water, produced gratuitously by the internal fires of the globe. A cold bath is impossible; but at six every evening I get into

(3)

a deep stone tank of blazing hot water and float in it until it is more Shaw soap or G.B. essence, and I come out a mere bone smelling powerfully of sulphur. Streams of hot water run about everywhere; and the vegetation is that of an open-air hothouse. Charlotte likes the place and has turned on a bad throat to justify a stay of four days. I shall use up the extra five days by making a third dash into the desert to Bou Saada. If I never reappear, conclude that I have stuck in the sand. I am due at Southampton on the 3rd. May.

G.B.S.

(1)

We are again in the desert at Bou Saada. It was represented to us as rather an adventure to try the road here; but it was much better than the road to Biskra; and the worst-spoken-of stretch of it was like a racecourse. There is nothing to do here; but the drives through the desert are very pleasant. As to mirage, the way here bangs everything I have seen in that line. Not merely lakes, but wonderful seas with coasts, headlands, islands rising out of mirror waters into

(2)

fairy clouds, surrounded us. One lake with a particularly fresh meadow on its banks was as near as 6 telegraph posts off: it was not until we reached that sixth post and found the desert still scorched and barren that Straker believed—or rather disbelieved —at last. We also had two bursts and a bad time repairing them. Our tyres are giving out, and we are 189 miles from new ones, which may prove serious tomorrow, when we start for Algiers via Aumale, where we break the journey. From Algiers, on the 28th., we sail with (or against) the gale, through the Bay of Biscay O!

G.B.S.

The building referred to on the following postcard is the cavalry barracks at Aumale.

26 April 1909.

This building is the dominating factor in Algeria; but the Arab doesnt care. At El Hanel we had coffee with the Marahout. Charlotte & Mrs. Cholmondely asked to pay respects to his wives. His reply (translated by the schoolmaster) was that he deeply regretted that the man who had the key of them was away at present.

G.B.S.

Not long after they got back home a new situation arose that fully engaged Shaw's energies. Performances of his play, The

Shewing-up of Blanco Posnet, *had been announced by the After Noon Theatre at His Majesty's Theatre, starting 4 June, but the play was forbidden by the censor. This aroused Shaw and with him the deeply-felt resentment to the censorship that had been increasing since the banning of Barker's* Waste *the previous year, and the Prime Minister, Mr. Asquith, appointed a Joint Select Committee of both Houses of Parliament to enquire into the working of the censorship, which started its meetings on 29 July. The following letter refers to press correspondence on the subject after the play had been banned. J. B. Fagan started his career as an actor in F. R. Benson's company in 1895, but retired from the stage for business and then became well known as a dramatic author and theatrical manager. In 1918 he took over the management of the Court Theatre where he produced* Heartbreak House *in 1921.*

Ayot St. Lawrence, Welwyn, Herts.

1st June 1909.

I have a sort of feeling that Fagan's letter in The Times ought to be answered: and I have scribbled the answer I might make if it were desirable for me to spoil the effect of my ten inch gun with a wretched little pistol shot. But it clearly isnt; so I dont send it. However, why shouldnt *you* have a go? Use my stuff as a draft to modify after what flourish your nature will.

If you dont, send it back to me, as it may come in handy somewhere. I feel that if we make the case against Redford as black as it really is, and leave it to be implied that he does it out of pure cussedness nobody will believe us. We must shew how he arrives at it with the best intentions.

G.B.S.

The story of the meetings of the Joint Committee and Shaw's part in the affair has been told elsewhere and there is no need to repeat it here. He had provided the heaviest fire in the battle, and his attack had encountered the heaviest resistance. Shaw had been taken off by his wife to Ireland again and from there he wrote the following postcard to Barker upon another matter. John Bull's Other Island *was still on tour, and Barker was*

155

bothered about William Poel's playing of Keegan. The new play was Misalliance.

Great Southern Hotel,
Parknasilla.

All you have to do with J. B.'s O. I. is to keep Poel *shouting*. Sit in the back row of the pit and yell whenever a word drops: nothing else is needed: the play will impose itself by itself. Also, do not disparage Nigel's clowning: on the contrary buy him a new red hot poker. Sempre ffff is the word.

I have begun a play—only three days at it so far. Something like Getting Married in construction. Hall Caine has done a heroic screed against the Censor: he will be the best of the bunch, like all new converts.

G.B.S.

In the next letter Shaw returns to the censorship. Lord Gorell, Lord Newton and the Earl of Plymouth were members of the committee which had recently resumed its meetings after a month's adjournment. Hall Caine had just given evidence opposing the censorship: Shaw's preface to Hall Caine's novel The White Prophet *was written to secure the novelist's support. The Scottish business was Alfred Wareing's Scottish National Theatre Company. Shaw always expressed a high opinion of Barker's* The Marrying of Ann Leete.

Southern Hotel, Parknasilla
2nd October 1909.

I have just fired what I hope will be my last shot in the Censor battle for the present—a colossal letter to The Times. Pretext: the arrival of the license for B. Posnet, with all the old omissions endorsed.

Incidentally I have given Gorell apoplexy, Newton beans, and Plymouth his quietus. Especially Gorell. Ha! Ha! Talk of personalities!

I also formed a combination with Hall Caine (who was going to support Censorship). I have written a smashing preface to The White Prophet—so smashing that the D. Telegraph didnt

156

dare publish it—and given H.C. the Occupation's head on a charger.

At last we are getting combined. Pinero and the Dramatists Club, the Sub. Com^{tee} of the Authors, and now Hall Caine. If I can only keep you youths from turning up your noses and your elders from delighting to bark and bite, we shall presently have something like a profession.

When the committee's report was issued on the following 11 November, a compromise solution to the problem of the censorship was put forward, which was not, however, followed by any change in the law.

4

Repertory

The last letter, dated 2 October 1909, breaks off to touch upon another subject, Barker's projected visit to Glasgow to help Wareing's Scottish Repertory Theatre.

2 October 1909

I think this Glasgow business is folly. They should have pulled through (if Glasgow really wants them) on Arms and the Man. Besides you want rest and petting. When it comes to your writing a letter to Charlotte beginning "Is it wise" things are serious. Mon, twas an awfu' mistake.

Archer is a hopeless Philistine. I read Ann Leete again and am more fascinated than ever by it. W.A. might as well complain that a Gainsborough isnt a Haydon or a Hilton. Courtney too! grumbling because you havent been sympathetic to the whore.

Why dont you write a preface? It belongs to the school.

The play, now longer than Getting Married, has at last reached Lillah's entrance—consequently not yet the beginning of the play.

Back on Friday.

G.B.S.

Barker was still unwell, but he gave support to the Glasgow scheme. He had published his Three Plays *without preface or portrait despite Shaw's urgings.* Misalliance, *intended for Lillah McCarthy, was getting on, but Shaw returns to the proposed Glasgow visit and the idea that Barker should play Tanner in* Man and Superman *there.*

M. & S. is not a bit of use without a really considerable Ann. If Lillah will get up and go, there may be something in it, but such a performance as Wareing can scrape together for a week will not do him any good or you any good (bar the immediate cash) or the play any good. And to flourish your conviction that Ann doesnt matter and never did matter is most unhygienic just at present. The physical strain on you would also be very considerable, though the mere change might do you good. Your provincial reputation is the most important asset you have; and you ought not to flatten it out by appearing in second rate productions, as this will inevitably be. Wareing might just as well put up Harben as Tanner if he hasnt an adequate Ann—or Lloyd. Like all Romeos you think Juliet doesnt matter; but she does. If Wareing will engage Fred Terry and Julia Neilson he may get his money back; but to get you alone for £50. is folly: a ten pound Tanner will do just as well for a "literarie success" as Trebitsch calls it. What have you to urge against all this?

G.B.S.

Shaw now refers to Barker's salary for playing Tanner in Glasgow; but the performances did not take place until the following September. The play Shaw had just finished was Misalliance. *He wanted Lillah McCarthy but she was not available. "Judy" was his secretary. He had written the play very quickly, for he had started it only at the end of September. The reference to Barrie is to his domestic trouble.*

Ayot St. Lawrence, Welwyn, Herts.
4th. Nov. 1909.

You have no more consideration for that unfortunate Wareing than if you had never been inside a repertory theatre in your life. You know quite well that £50 would be sheer robbery—I come up tomorrow afternoon for the Fabian Committee—I have just finished the play (first draft); and if Lillah wont do the necessary gymnastics for me (the part is one of a professional athlete) I shall want Violet Vanbrugh. Also Weedon Grossmith.

Also Clarence. Also somebody for a big B.B. sort of part—the Amorous Linendraper. Also Mona Limerick. Also Loraine. Also a good old woman: possibly Florence Haydon, but perhaps something vulgarar. Also some little squit of a nervous boy who can cry and scream like a burlesque of Eugene. I only want one scene, as in Getting Married. Properties: a portable Turkish bath and an aeroplane. Frohman, who expects a melodrama, will be dumbfounded and will most likely throw up the whole affair.

If Judy works hard enough at extending the shorthand, a reading may be possible by the middle of next week—you can come down here for it if your Barrie will let you. Why didn't you tell me about him? I had to get it all from Marshall at the Dramatists' lunch, which you should have attended. You can bring him to hear the play if you like; but it will lacerate his soul. Charlotte wants to know the address of the guilty pair, to invite them to lunch.

G.B.S.

The three following postcards deal with the casting of Misalliance, *which was to be the second production by the Frohman Repertory Theatre, now actively being prepared for.*

[Postmarked Dec. 29 09]

I dont expect any difficulty whatever about Loraine and Tarleton: but I may shortly doubt whether he will throw himself into the repertory company to be cast for anything you please. We will have to humor him, because there is really no alternative to him: C.V.C. would be no use. I'm afraid Loraine is too hard and British for Constantine; but his strength would be useful. Craig being off, Constantine is a serious difficulty. Pity Delph hasn't the nerve for it. Playfair would be ideal if you could only see Omar Khayyamity. He is precisely the man. Then there's Ainley—Muraddin and the Fair Persian. And Hignett. I have no lists here unluckily. Martin Harvey? H. B. Irving, of course, but you couldn't get him. The play has gone to the printers; and as soon as they get it through we shall be ready for Redford. If he throws us back on revivals we shall want Farren and Eric Lewis.

The Bull, Burnley. 31/12/09.
(Back to Edstaston tomorrow)

Naif! You do not understand. The £90 is to bribe him not to go into management himself with Marie Löhr as his leading lady. It will have to be paid anyhow, Tarleton or no Tarleton. We may as well have the benefit of it.

Stella has not the drive, the zest for Hypatia. If we have to postpone, Mona may be available.

Scotch printers drink out the old, drink in the new, except for that there will be no delay, as there is no pressure of printing work just now.

G.B.S.

[Postmarked Jan. 1 1910.]

Mona Limerick says she could begin to rehearse in London on the 7th March: that is the best she can do.

I have often pointed out Guy's qualities to you—he is so like Sir William Collins of the L.C.C. A possible Bohun, even a possible Ridgeon, but NOT a possible Tarleton.

It looks as if I should not be back until the 9th—to Ayot. Also as if I were destined to be the Easter attraction.

Last night I spoke for 2½ hours at 2 successive meetings; and the hotel staff saw the New Year in with dancing and noisy revelry until 5 in the morning, when I went to sleep until 7.30 and then got up to drive through 50 miles of hilly trammy industrial district.

G.B.S.

Bentleys Hotel, Merthyr Tydfil,
until Thursday morning.
[Postmarked 24 Jan. 1910.]

I am writing to Loraine to ask whether he is really unattainable. Marie Lohr may be engaged where she likes; the point is that she and R.L. could start a theatre tomorrow and get all Maugham's plays; and the salaries paid to prevent that must not be charged in full against the repertory scheme. As to W., of course he could play Tarleton or Constantine. So could Valentine, just as well. You have V: why engage W? I shouldn't be in a hurry: it is only the 4th Jan, too soon for counsels of despair.

G.B.S.

Barker wanted a list of members of the Stage Society and the Fabian Society to circularise on behalf of the Frohman Repertory and got the following answer from Shaw.

10, Adelphi Terrace,
London, W.C.
19th January 1910.

There is a list of the members of the Stage Society in the Reports, which I suppose you have. If not, I presume it is to be had for the asking: probably Whelen has used it for his After Noon Theatre.

As to getting the Fabian Society's list, that must not be done. Cases have arisen of people being victimized for belonging to the Society; and the most solemn resolutions have been made never to let the lists out of our hands. The utmost you can do is to induce Pease to let you have the addressed envelopes on your solemn pledge not to make a list from them. You could then compare them with the other envelopes and reject the duplicates. Of course there is always the alternative of facing the overlapping. I got no less than five circulars from Fisher Unwin the other day. He was apparently working from five lists or directories. But the effect is certainly annoying, and gives the impression of bad organization.

There is no mortal reason why the Court Theatre list should not be used: quite the contrary. If we went back to the Court next year, we should do all the better for having kept our sheep fed in the interval. I daresay V.D. "refrained" from using the list for Waller; but even Vedrenne, in his stagiest moments, could hardly pretend that this was an act of self-denial. Why the devil should he send an appeal to the Court clientele for The Three Musketeers and so forth? However, there can be no objection to our accepting the list as an act of magnanimity on his part so long as we get it.

I am going down to Ayot this afternoon, and shall not return until Friday just before the Publishing Committee. I am happy to say that I am getting through a headache: I was afraid it would wait until the beginning of rehearsals, which would have been very inconvenient.

G.B.S.

H. Granville Barker, Esq.,
The Duke of York's Theatre.

The reader may, if he pleases, amuse himself by identifying the players mentioned by Shaw under their initials, in the following communication—a not very difficult task.

Ayot St. Lawrence,
Welwyn, Herts.
Jan. 20th 1910.

As to C.L., I really think you had better see a doctor. What conceivable use would she be for Hypatia? If I saw George F. in Brassbound that time in Fulham I won't have him at any price. If we can't get N.F. we had better have Esmond if he can be depended on. I shall be at Adelphi Terrace from 4 to 5 on Friday, and can see anyone you send then; but I shall hold on to D.B. unless he extricates himself very resolutely: it is just right for him. If M.L. cannot be had, we had better try Rosalind Ivan. I should venture with the Smiler if she were just a little more downright and less elusive; but impatient audacity is not her line. However, as Trench does not appreciate M.L. probably he will let her go.

G.B.S.

The following is contained on eight picture postcards. Shaw is occupied with Fabian affairs, and the Society of Authors, which was his trade union, and with the Frohman Repertory. Shaw's statement of the situation with Frohman is clear. The repertory had started on 21 February with John Galsworthy's Justice, *followed by Shaw's* Misalliance *and Barker's* The Madras House, *all of which, after 26, 11 and 10 performances respectively, had been dropped.*

(1)

I am now getting close in, and am pretty sure of being in London on Monday up to time for Webb's meeting, if not for the Authors' Society's committee of management, which meets on that afternoon. I have not written a word of anything dramatic —nothing but reports of hotels for the Royal Automobile Club. We are all exhausted and demoralized. Charlotte positively loathes me, and is, as usual pathetically unable to

(2)

dissimulate. Mrs. Chumly keeps in good humor and even in good spirits, in spite of asthma, sore throat, and a bad cold in the head. Even Kilsby, sleeping in damp sheets every night, is off color. Every morning I feel as if I had had a drunken debauch the night before; but when I get up and out, my energy returns; and I drive off and dash into churches and round the towns as if I really had something at stake in them from the mere habit of energy. Another month of

(3)

it and I should drop dead in the middle of some such burst of false activity. What they all want, poor dears, is a holiday from *me,* though they don't know it.

I got your letter at Chartres, where the stained glass is more wonderful than ever. This was the second letter. I got the first at Albi. I cannot make out what you are producing. What is Helena's

(4)

Path, or Pathé (it suggests a cinematograph show?)

As to Permeation versus Secession, we have no choice in the matter. We did not undertake to compete: we undertook to propagate a higher drama. Producing a lot of plays merely to ascertain which draws the most money, and running that and dropping the rest is not Propagandist Repertory: it is

(5)

competitive commerce pure and simple, and can end only in a theatre for second hand plays, exploiting revivals of old successes. The announced program cannot now be carried out, because it includes several revivals of my plays, which I shall not permit, as, if they proved pecuniarily successful Frohman would simply run them to death, and if they did as Misalliance did, he would drop them as failures. Therefore, no more Shaw at the R.P. It is up to you to say whether there is to be any more Barker; for they will

(6)

presently want Voysey; and if you let them have it, a month or so will see the end of it for the next ten years one way or the other, just as it will see the end of Trelawney. Charles has not played the game for a single moment. I dont blame him, I don't see how any manager who has the other game open to him as an alternative *can* play our game, but that does not alter the facts: the R.T. is not an

(7)

R.T. in our sense; and all we have succeeded in doing is to prove the impossibility of a high class theatre under a commercial management. We have also demonstrated before hand what the National Theatre will be if it ever gets founded; and the moral is that we must revive Vedrenne and Barker (even if VD is Whelen or another as he must be if he goes on with this silly nonsense about Lillah) in a theatre where £600 a week gate money will cover expenses. It is no [use]

(8)

pretending that we can draw more or that we ever did draw more. We should have gone into the Court Theatre figures scientifically, and extracted the averages: we have never yet looked them in the face. The expenses at the D. of Y's are gamblers' expenses and F's financial habits gamblers' habits. Neither will do for us. Secession is finally inevitable; and you had better not sacrifice another play—especially Voysey—to keep the D. of Y's going. I shall make no secret of the fact that I am out of it, and that the promised revivals are off.

G.B.S.

After eleven weeks the end of the Repertory Theatre was in sight as the following letter confirms. The repertory ended on

17 June. Shaw was highly displeased at Misalliance's *mere eleven performances.*

Ayot St. Lawrence, Welwyn, Herts.
9th May 1910.

The bolt has fallen on Frohman. Yesterday I got a letter about Major Barbara in America which compelled me to bring matters to a point, as Charles has been holding up my plays (especially Blanco and Barbara) without, as fas as I can see, the smallest serious purpose concerning them. So I wrote to him that the Shaw-Frohman combination is off—that he is not a bit of use to me, nor I to him, and that I must make other plans both for London and America. He may not realize at once that this is the immutable truth and that his power stops at the commercial frontier; but it is so: there is nothing to be done with him now. Trebitsch, whose wife is a parffic lidy and very nice, wants you to get your plays translated by Julius Bab—a good idea.

G.B.S.

Ayot St. Lawrence, Welwyn, Herts.
10th May 1910.

This is his way of saying that he is chucking the Repertory altogether, as from now; also the devil (meaning you and me) and all his works for ever and ever.

And now, what's the next move?

G.B.S.

I shall be in London on Thursday and Friday.

Shaw had been ready for a Shaw-Frohman combination not only in London but in America, for Frohman had seen (in America) what profits Shaw could bring to the theatre, but he had no idea of what the dramatist was driving at either in his plays or in his way of presenting them, and such a combination was out of the question.

Barker was deeply disappointed at the failure of the repertory, which had, however, everything against it: an unsuitable theatre, no real policy, and a manager whose entire outlook was against what was required to nurse such an enterprise into success. For the sake of his work he thought of going to Germany and becoming a naturalized member of a nation that took the theatre more seriously than did the English.

In the summer of 1910 the Shaws were again on holiday in Ireland, where they stayed with Lady Gregory. He wrote a lament to Barker on five picture postcards on the holiday and his increasing age.

26th July 1910.

MY 54th BIRTHDAY

(1)

Charlotte has just reminded me very unnecessarily of the above ghastly fact. After all, it has been a fine day, which is something considering that on our landing at Belfast on Sunday morning it rained hard for 36 hours, causing a steady rise in Charlotte's temper. In that downpour we drove round the Antrim coast to the Giants Causeway. In that downpour I sat

(2)

under my umbrella in my aquascutum, like a putrid mushroom, whilst a drenched mariner rowed me round the cliffs and told me lies about them. In that downpour we drove back next day to Lough Bay, only to find the hotel too revolting to pass the night in. In that downpour we pushed on to Antrim, only to find two hotels there so loathsome that we simply turned tail and returned to Belfast where the hotel we didnt go to (Charlotte at the last moment consented to stay at the Grand Central after heaping insults

(3)

on the manager and ordering the instant repacking of all the luggage) was burnt to the ground with some slaughter and much concussion of the brain through the people who jumped out casting themselves from the third floor head foremost. Today the sun reappeared; and we came across the mountains—mountains I had never heard of; the Sperrin—to Londonderry, where Charlotte, as aforesaid, reminded me that I am 54. Here men still chalk up on the walls "No surrender" and "No Popery," with

(4)

XVIII century dates attached. And here they preserve the old

167

walls: and you mount them to look out at the place where the besieged Protestant heroes once watched the relief ships breaking the boom across the Foyle, and discover, as you may see from this card, that nothing whatever can be seen from the walls now except the hideous houses that have been built outside them. The ugliness of these towns, and the slightness of the provocation on which the inhabitants raise up their voices and call one another sanguinary liars

(5)

is quite astonishing. Yet, like Larry Doyle, they are civil to strangers. In this Northern Counties Hotel there is an apparently young and lovely spaniel. I have just discovered that it is blind and 18 years old. Possibly I shall find a letter from you at Rosapenna tomorrow. Fifty-four is a devil of an age. I cannot feel it—cannot believe it; and yet there is the repulsive mask. Fifty four! *Fifty* four! Well!

G.B.S.

The Imperial Hotel, Enniskillen,
Lough Erne.
9 August 1910.

I am writing by this post to the bank for money and must wait for the reply until Friday morning here. This is to warn you that we had a quite Pyrenean disappointment at the Dowros Bay Hotel & fled leaving all our arrangements for forwarding letters in confusion. We are without money or clean clothes, & have been turned out, or rather crowded out of Bundoran (a beastly Irish Biarritz) after one night's shelter. A commercial hotel in the main street of Enniskillen now makes much of us. Charlotte's self control is, under the circumstances, heroic; but she takes it out in insults to the hotel people.

G.B.S.

The Coronet proposal mentioned in the following letter was one of many ideas for reviving the glories of the Court at the Coronet Theatre, Notting Hill Gate, and Barker was dallying with it; but it came to nothing and he played John Tanner in Glasgow in Alfred Wareing's repertory company.

c/o Lady Gregory, Coole Park, Gort.
Co. Galway.
20th August 1910.

Just getting over a most fearful headache. The whole difficulty about this Coronet business is its outrageous suddenness and offhandedness. A revival of the Court scheme is simply the most valuable theatrical goodwill in London—indeed the *only* one existing; and the Coronet, with its suburban prices (I hope they are not to be raised: if so, I wont look at the scheme) is just the right opening; but Arthur should have made a well considered three years proposal months ago, instead of jumping up this silly snatch at a stopgap with a demand for an answer within ten days in the middle of August. Nothing is really possible except Misalliance, which would draw all the people who missed it at the Dukes, and give Lillah a good show. But it must be announced and played for at least four weeks whether it draws or not.

I bar Man & Superman at the Coronet. It is played out on the old lines; and a revival would add nothing to your or it's reputation and would be too stale to add much to my income. I shall save it up for Loraine now. Glasgow is another matter. I have no objection to Wareing's project; but a share of profits is not much to the point where profits do not occur; and an appearance in Glasgow for L. is not an appearance in London. Still, it is Misalliance at the Coronet or M. & S. in Glasgow: take your choice. You should play Summerhays Senr, and Madras should be revived too to defy the Press.

G.B.S.

The following letter refers to another Frederick Whelen scheme for "repertory," which did not come off.

Ayot St. Lawrence, Welwyn, Herts.
13th Dec. 1910.

The charming letter is a fiction. I havent written anything of the kind since I saw you last.

The Advisory Board, if I joined it, would bring down on me all the actors out of engagement in England, and all the unacted authors as well. Every rehearsal of a play would be laid to my door. And I should be bound by the votes of a majority of the Board.

If I remain simply a modest author I escape all this; and my real power, which consists in the indispensability of my plays to the enterprise, remains intact.

As your position is the same as mine, I advise you to do likewise. I told Whelen he might say that he was on good terms with me and could virtually secure my plays, but that I could not take any official part in the enterprise.

G.B.S.

The Shaws went on a cruise to Jamaica, where they stayed with Sir Sydney Olivier, the Governor, and he sends Barker a greeting.

Kings House, Jamaica.
11th Jan. 1911.

It is a lovely morning. I am wearing the Superman suit, Act III. I am taking photographs in 100th of a second through yellow screens or watching the lizards and dragon flies. The morning coolness is delightful: it is not much above 70 in the shade. Charlotte (in a padded dressing gown) is quite happy. Olivier's new poet-earthquake palace of reinforced concrete is a masterpiece of *nouveau* art. The trees and mountains look pleasantly theatrical through the mosquito curtains when one wakes in the morning. On the whole it was a good move this. The voyage was 14 days, and only 3 of them tropical: the rest rough and rolling, especially 36 hours of rolling to 45° on New Years Day, but I got my sea legs in 48 hours and did quite a lot of reading and writing. I shall arrive in London simultaneously with this letter.

G.B.S.

When he got back from Jamaica, Shaw had to clear up his affairs with the business of Vedrenne-Barker, which had finally come to an end. Shaw's letter to Vedrenne shows that the management ended in debt, which Shaw had to bear, and it shows too how he treated the matter, despite the distress suffered by his financially sensitive soul.

170

10, Adelphi Terrace, W.C.
1st March 1911.

My dear V.D.

My solicitors are clear and unanswerable as to the balance sheet. Your accountants proceeded on the erroneous assumption that I am a partner. I am not: I am a creditor. Everything belongs to me, cash in bank, scenery, library, band parts, the Royalty Theatre, Circus Road, Phyllis, the boy, everything that you and Barker possess up to the value of £5,250. Barker takes nothing, because, being a partner, he cannot rank as a creditor.

I attach some importance to the cash, and a great deal to Phyllis, whose consent, however, is (by an oversight in the law) necessary to her transfer to my household. If she refuses, I sweep away the house, the boy, the theatre, the furniture, plate, linen, and everything except what you stand in. To place her in the dilemma was my real object in lending the money and writing plays for V. & B. The mask is now off: she must yield or bring about the ruin of all that is dear to her. Could Melville devise such a plot?

Lillah, it seems, is going to succeed Gertrude Kingston at the Little Theatre . . .

Yours ever,
G. Bernard Shaw.

This was followed by a further letter:

I have received from you a cheque for £484: 3: 10 being the amount of cash in bank to the credit of the firm of Vedrenne & Barker at the moment of remittance. I await a further payment of the amount to be realized by the sale of the firm's scenery and other assets. In the meantime, I undertake to accept these payments as a full discharge of the indebtedness of the firm of Vedrenne & Barker to me in respect of the sum of £5250 advanced by me to them; and in the event of my decease before a final settlement, you may treat this letter as such a discharge.

[Signed over a penny stamp.]

5

The Lillah McCarthy-Granville
Barker Management

In the meantime, as Shaw has said, Lillah McCarthy had gone into management at the Little Theatre, with Granville Barker as producer, opening on 11 March, 1911 with Barker's version of Anatol. *What made the management possible was Shaw's* Fanny's First Play, *which was put on, after only a fortnight's rehearsal, on Wednesday 19 April. Here was the first Shaw play to open the eyes of the playgoer, accustomed to everyday West End theatrical fare, to the possibility that the Shavian drama was for him. It had a rapturous reception, not in the least diminished by the pretence that the play was not, perhaps, by Bernard Shaw. With this play Shaw joined the ranks of the long-run playwrights, not willingly, but because once started he could not stop its run, which continued at the Little Theatre till the end of the year, afterwards at the Kingsway Theatre for a total of 624 performances.*

When he handed the play to the new actress-manager, Shaw was emphatic that its authorship was not to be disclosed. Let people think the play is by Barrie, he said. Mystification as to its authorship would add to the talk about it, he considered, and undoubtedly there was much discussion, though why anyone should have been deceived is not easy to see. Shaw rehearsed the play, as usual, and his rehearsal notes on green paper are in existence.

The Shaws afterwards went on holiday to the Continent.

After achieving an almost inconceivable headache at Amiens, here I am, spending the night in an inn. Fine weather and forty miles an hour have revived me somewhat; but two first-class headaches within ten days is beyond reason. Decidedly I must be breaking up. Have you finished that play yet? Dont suppose you will live for ever or that you can improve the quality of the water of life by pouring too much into each bucket.

G.B.S.

Barker worked ceaselessly at his plays, never satisfied, and the one referred to on the above postcard was never completed: it was to have been called The Wicked Man. *Two days later Shaw sent him a postcard from Rheims with a picture of the statue of Jeanne d'Arc, on which he wrote:*

Charlotte thinks this strikingly like you.
Ha! Ha!
Ho! Ho!
Lord help her!

G.B.S.

The Prime Minister entertained their Majesties in connection with the Coronation celebrations of King George V and Queen Mary when it was proposed to perform at 10 Downing Street Shaw's The Man of Destiny *and Barrie's* The Twelve-Pound Look, *and Shaw wrote the following postcard to Lillah McCarthy who was to play in each.*

Chateau de Coucy.
21/6/11
How are you getting on with the Strange Lady? Dont bother finessing about her: you wont get it that way. Play the downright aristocrat when the lady is not deliberately acting: go in for strength and beauty rather than for Lamballesque elegance. You havnt time to study a period: at such short notice all you can do is to fling on the stage a straight playing of the part in your own manner.

I am sorry I couldnt come in to rehearsal of Fanny on Monday:
as it was, we did not get away until 3 o/clock.

G.B.S.

*In fact, when the performance was given on 30 June an act
from* John Bull's Other Island *was substituted for the Napoleon
play. Shaw mentions the matter in the letter that follows. The
King's private secretary, Sir Arthur John Bigge, who the same year
became Baron Stamfordham, was a man of vast experience of
royalty, and no doubt remembered how greatly his late master,
Edward VII, had enjoyed the Irish play:*

Grand Hotel Du Lac
Garardmer, Vosges.
27th June 1911.

Just got your letter. Couldnt be better for you and me. The
M. of D. was an idiotic selection; & Bigge & Co. have played into
our hands, as they naturally would in their hopeless ignorance
of their own game. I cannot honestly say that you did so well
for Lillah as you did for me. Nora does not exactly dominate
that third act, but she will leave a pleasant impression as a
colleen (she can be as young and lovely as she likes) and she
will have the £12 L to star in. And there will be nobody else
in the leading lady line. Nevertheless I feel some remorse at
having stolen so much of her command night. I cant help thinking
that the Sign of the Cross would have given more satisfaction.

I dont approve of Genoa. The cholera is at last admitted to be
serious: a man who just smelt Naples has died of it. When will
the Galsworthies be at Costina.

G.B.S.

*Elizabeth Marbury mentioned in the following letters was an
American agent. Lee Shubert was a New York manager (with
his brother J. J.) and had his own theatre. Shaw outlines an
ambitious scheme for Barker to consider, writing with an eye to
business, and so advises his friend.*

Hotel Beau Rivage, Annecy, Haute Savoie, France.

6th July 1911.

As Charlotte likes this place and there are plenty of mountainous excursions within reach, we shall stay here another week—say until the 13th. unless you hear to the contrary.

Miss Marbury telegraphs that Shubert wants Fanny, and offers to engage you to produce it. I have replied that my terms would be as usual; but what does Barker say?

What *do* you say? For my part I have no faith in this sort of snapping up of reputed successes by ignoramuses. It means simply slaughter unless you go out; and it is silly to go out for one job—silly of Shubert to do it in that helpless way, I mean. If you do this sort of thing at all, you should go out with a repertory and a company, beginning with a tour of the big towns in the United Kingdom (or ending with it) and including about 6 plays, 3 of yours and 3 of mine. It remains to be seen whether the Little Theatre can grow such a company and repertory for us; but if it could, the touring would finance the theatre (if it needed it) and become an institution. The old game is up, I think; and the local repertory theatres will never be able to handle the current output of the higher drama otherwise than provisionally. We must get a steady living out of our plays or else abandon the theatre altogether. Here are you, the author of Voysey, Madras, Ann Leete (to mention no other masterpieces) and what, I ask you, do you get out of them? Where should I be if I had to live on my tantiemes? Not in Annecy, I trow. Camden Town, more likely.

Consider this when Elizabeth Marbury approaches you. She lately tempted me with a golden offer from an enthusiast in the Shubertian line who sent me his prompt copy of the Doctor's Dilemma as arranged by him for the stage. All the lines without which the funny lines would not be funny were completely scored out. The entire fifth act, except "Then I have committed a perfectly disinterested murder," which was transferred to the curtain at the end of act four, was eliminated by a masterstroke of blue pencil. It is lunacy to leave our plays to these excellent creatures: the better they mean, the more disastrous they are.

I do not know whether Judy keeps you posted in my address: if she does, I may hear from you tomorrow. Make a note that on the 8th. July, Judy goes to The Cottage, Smarden, S.O. Kent for her villeggiaturel but Mrs. Bilton, at the Terrace, will have the earliest news of my whereabouts, as I always wire to Adelphi. As far as I can make out, letters posted in London before 6 p.m. reach this part of France on the morning of the next day but one.

I want news of Lillah as The Dainty Dish ("set before a king") as I suppose I ought to write to Mrs. Asquith about it.

I have a cranky sort of notion of a play—a Superman play—with a heroine of 55. My female contemporaries are in great need of it.

Also three good historical sketches for Moss Empires.

But I have written nothing on this tour except a scrap of a preface for the new edition of the Quintessence of Ibsenism. That is the worst of it: I have such a devil of a lot of odd jobs to finish.

G.B.S.

Grenoble.
12 July 1911.

I am now quite muddled as to Shubert and Fanny. Miss Marbury sends me the usual agent's notion of an agreement (total rights of Fanny for Canada and the U.S. for 5 years) which I have thrown into the waste paper basket. I take it that you are to see Shubert and tell him that this notion of picking up Fanny as a London success and exploiting it in the usual way is no good and that we decide (as per your recent but probably by this time forgotten letter) to wait until the L.T. has been at work a little longer and offer him a reputation and a repertory company for an American Tour.

Tomorrow we move to Chamonix: this place is a blast furnace, & Kilsby is down to ten stone eight and has no nose to speak of—all peeled off.

G.B.S.

Robert Loraine opened with Man and Superman *at the Criterion Theatre on 29 September with Pauline Chase as Ann. On the 15th of the month Shaw sent a picture postcard from Rennes to Lillah McCarthy on which he said, referring to the proposal:*

I am informed by Loraine that Miss Pauline Chase is to be the new Ann Whitefield. What on earth is she like? I have been refusing all his suggestions for years, and am only too glad now to accept somebody whom I dont *know* to be impossible—not having seen her. Send me a line to Adelphi.

He had already written to Barker at length about Loraine's proposal which, despite Shaw's doubts, opened as proposed. Fanny *was by no means dead at the Little Theatre, so that* The Doctor's Dilemma *was not done there, neither was the* Madras House *nor* Misalliance *revived.* Fanny *was a cheap play for a little theatre, and the other plays were not.*

Metropolitan Hotel, Tours.
11th Sept. 1911.

I have just had a telegram from Loraine to say that he has taken the Criterion Theatre from the 29th. and proposes to play Man and Superman there with Pauline Chase as Ann, and the rest of the cast our old lot, except that he names Doris Lytton as Violet. I know nothing about her. For that matter I know nothing about Miss P.C., whom I vaguely conceive to be an ambitious columbine who played Peter Pan and takes flights in aeroplanes. There is no reason for her taking a flight in Man and Superman; but I am not indisposed to experiment with her, because the situation of holding up Man and Superman in London for R.L. is not really a long sustainable one; and the sooner it is ended by letting him have his fling the better. He cannot very well open on the 29th., even with Miss Haydon, Casson, Lloyd, Beveridge, Agnes Thomas, Gwenn and Barnes (who know the parts and the business) because the theatre is in such a condition that I shall have to insist on heavy repairs and spring cleanings. Also I shall make him hand over the scenery to Norman Wilkinson & make one or two alterations in the cast, besides perhaps waiting for me to look in at the final rehearsals. But on the whole, though I have not yet consented, and have vehemently protested against having the claim jumped in my absence, I foresee that I shall let him try it, though he has evidently been let into a bad bargain. Except as an aviator he is old fashioned: he has no notion how completely the palmy days of the Criterion have passed away; and he still thinks that M. & S. never had a real chance in London because it wasnt done in that palmy way. Of course it is possible that he may carry it through by his vitality and impetuosity and congenital stage power in spite of (he will think because of) the reversion to methods that are still apparently in full vogue in America, and also because he has had no real success as a galvaniser of box office plays, and is very far from being as pigheaded in his inherited convictions and his conscientious desire to be always perfectly smart as I am in *my* artistic convictions. Besides, if the attempt proves a throw away, it is only a throw-away of the chance I promised him, not of the play. On the whole, as I should like to please him; as he plays the part extraordinarily well and ought to have another chance of shewing what he can do with it in London: and—as aforesaid—as I have a strong disinclination (the result of early experience with Candida) ever again to hold up a play for anybody. I fall back on Webb's principle that "better is the enemy of well" and resolve to let the thing go through if my conditions are complied with.

All this by way of apology for the idiocy of the whole affair— the wrong theatre—the wrong everything that makes atmosphere —the wrong moment as far as my absence is concerned.

Clare Greet writes for her old part in The Doctor. Does this mean that you have announced it, & that Fanny is dead at last? Tomorrow I move on to Angers (Hotel Cheval Blanc), where we *must* stay at least 2 nights to get our clothes washed, and where I shall receive a budget of letters.

I am cool about the Doctor. It comes back to me again and again that we should revive Madras and Misalliance and refuse to accept the Frohman defeat. The houses that sickened him would fill the L.T.

The hotel attendants are undisguisedly anxious to see me go to bed; and it is desirable for my own sleep's sake that I should gratify them; so good night.

G.B.S.

Back in England Shaw was hard at work as usual, including public speaking. The postmarks on the following two picture postcards are undecipherable. The Dramatic Sub-Committee refers to the Society of Authors, and the Club is the Dramatists' Club. The "licensing" was the appointment of Charles Brookfield, a one-time popular dramatist, as Joint Examiner of Plays in November, 1911, a subject that rent the sub-committee.

Lichfield.

(1)

I am staying tonight (Tuesday) here on my way to the Potteries, where I have to lecture tomorrow. I shall stay at the North Stafford Station Hotel, Stoke upon Trent, though I have to lecture in Hanley. On Thursday I shall drive back to Ayot. On Friday morning I shall come up to town; so I shall be at the Dramatic Sub-Committee. I do not see exactly where they are likely to go wrong about the licensing; but I will shepherd them as best

(2)

I can if there is a stampede. Your neglect of the Sub Com^tee. is scandalous: you have no professional conscience. The club too, needs looking after. Now that Zangwill is on, and Mason, and that the Popular-Unimportants are getting tired of it and staying away, something might be done with it: at all events a watching brief is worth holding.

G.B.S.

Despite the protests, Brookfield's appointment as censor held good. The Barkers' unsatisfied ambition was to produce Shakespeare, with Shaw checking them; but at least he makes an important proposal to his friend—which was not carried out.

Ayot St. Lawrence, Welwyn, Herts.
13th Feb. 1912.

Here is a thing for you to consider.

All captures of the front rank of the profession are affected by a revival of Hamlet. The play revives sensationally every 15 years or so, with intermediate successes of esteem. Thus you have Irving and Forbes-Robertson, with Wilson Barrett or Tree in between. Neither W.B. nor Tree could touch I. & F.R. because they were personally incredible Hamlets.

Now F.R. was about 15 years ago. The hour has come for a new audible Hamlet; and in my opinion, a feature of the new one will be (as in Poel's Juliet) youthfulness. Having digested this, turn your eyes now to Moscow, where Teddy Craig has staged Hamlet (or induced the papers to say so). Why not collar Craig's production with Wilkinson, Ricketts, or another, and play Hamlet yourself? If Teddy would play the ghost of a lost soul (he could), all the better. Lillah, who is too big and strong for Orphelia, could make a new thing of the Queen, who has never had a chance so far. The cast should be carefully kept free from any flavour of the legitimate: for instance if Lauzerte could learn English, he would be right for the king.

Post here. Think it over.

G.B.S.

P.S. I shall be up on Friday.

The proposals contained in the following letters were in connection with the Kingsway Theatre to which the Barkers had moved at the end of the previous year. Barker had for some time been contemplating a visit to the United States with a number of plays.

Saracen's Head Hotel,
Lincoln.
Sunday, 21st April 1912.

Thus far.

I tried to pick up Cockerell at Cambridge for a couple of days; but Mrs. Douglas Cockerell, his sister-in-law is dead; and he is away on that business.

We—Judy and I—will leave here after lunch tomorrow, and stop somewhere short of York, possibly Doncaster. I hope to get to York early enough on Tuesday to telegraph for my letters. I shall telegraph my address to you also, and expect you to join us in York as early as may be.

As to Candida, I am not sure, considering that it has not been done in London for eight years, that it is wise to throw it away as a summer stopgap. No play put up in June has much of a chance: Candida has none. You had better do something flashier or do nothing. Why not let the theatre for July and August, or start a cinematograph? I suppose the difficulty is rehearsing the American plays. Anyhow, let us confer further. I seriously think we might try next time to get a bit of real business with Candida. It would be very profitable, the play being so cheap; and it might revive something of the old interest. If you want a stopgap, try You Never Can Tell, and send it on tour, the demand for it seems inexhaustible; and it is at present going in bits and scraps among all sorts of impossible people.

Janet wants to play Lady Cicely in Liverpool!

G.B.S.

Weatherbound in
Rigg's Windermere Hotel,
Windermere.
1st May 1912.

It seems to me that if you have to put up a fresh play, it would be insanely uneconomical not to make it a rehearsal for America. Also, other things being equal, it had better not be a play by me, as to follow a year of Shaw with yet another Shaw is not very repertorial. I should do a Barker if you can get the company for America; and as Voysey is, I suppose, the surest item for New York, you might as well put it on, though I think Madras would be better still. I have never got quite rid of my objection to accepting the Duke of York's condemnation of Madras and Misalliance: the business they did would pay at the Kingsway very well. Fanny has never drawn as much. In fact we have been losing money by Fanny considered as a substitute for the D. of Y. failures.

Misalliance with Pelissier, Heggie, and Lillah as the acrobat would be immense but then Lillah will not be available for America. So it looks like Voysey or Madras. We must play strong up-to-date cards.

Did I tell you that Farren is keen on going to America with you?

Lucy ought to have £10 for the next play. If someone offers him £15 or £20 for a fashionable run, even with the chance of a failure, he would hardly refuse it for the sake of £7 which is really less than he ought to have; but he would not throw away a more permanent £10. Not my business, of course; but since you ask me—! He would be a good Crampton in Y.N.C.T. or, for that matter, a good waiter or even Phil. He is a possible Summerhays in Misalliance, and could fake a tolerable Booth Voysey with his voice and a good make-up.

We did 104 miles between Carlisle and here, what with the Roman wall and another accidental detour. At one place, Alston, we reached the eternal snows. It was cold and sunless; and Judy's cold revived with fearful violence. We went to the aeroplanists' sheds again; no Gnosspelins, and Adams repairing a hole in his petrol tank. Flying just about to begin as usual—still in that condition.

Headache over, happily. Not so lumbago. Wet mist all day today: nothing to be done out of doors.

We shall be here for the Animated Pictures after all, as I shall devote a day to Buttermere and half a day to Coniston. That is, I shall be at this hotel until Friday morning, possibly until Saturday.

G.B.S.

Before anything was done about the American visit an important new development arose. Shakespeare became possible through a gift of £10,000 from Lord Lucas. This changed the situation in London for Barker and he was on the lookout for a theatre for the purpose, the Kingsway being regarded as too small. Furthermore, Shaw was wickedly attempting to tempt Barker away from Shakespeare and back to Shaw, with all this money available. So there was talk of the new play, Androcles and the Lion, *being done at the Queen's Theatre, which belonged to Alfred Butt. That was not to be, for there was another matter in Shaw's mind as the next letter discloses. "She" was Mrs. Patrick Campbell.*

Ayot St. Lawrence, Welwyn, Herts.
30th June 1912.

You will have to look sharp or she will snatch the Queen's out of your very jaws. Never did I make a greater sacrifice to friendship than in not warning her: for though I entered on the business with the most insolent confidence in my superiority to a dozen such Delilahs, I fell head over ears in love with her—violently and exquisitely in love—before I knew that I was thinking about anything but business. All yesterday I could think of nothing but a thousand scenes of which she was the heroine and I the hero. And I am on the verge of 56. There has never been anything so ridiculous, or so delightful, in the history of the world. On Friday we were together for an hour: we visited a lord; we drove in a taxi; we sat on a sofa in Kensington Square; and my years fell from me like a garment. I was in love for very nearly 36 hours; and for that be all her sins forgiven her!

Today Richard is himself again; and this word Love, which grey-beards call divine, be resident in men like one another and not in me: I am myself alone (William). All the same, if she gets at Butt before Tuesday she will but him no buts, but hang the theatre to her apron-strings like the kitchen scissors. Your chance is her dislike of negotiations with sordid syndicalists. She will try to get Aubrey Smith (whom I want for Pickering) as her man of business; and she will have to consult du Maurier (her substitute for Loraine, whom she dreads as he dreaded Lillah—Ha! ha! Nemesis!) before she decides on a theatre. This means delay; and in delay lies no plenty for her and for me if you can jump the claim at once.

Now if she can reduce me so easily, what chance has Frohman against her with Barrie? His virtue will be as wax, and melt in its own fires. Therefore, consider, good shepherd, whether, if the du Maurier combination fails, and no theatre is forthcoming, and Barrie can refuse her nothing, and you have the Queen's under God and Butt, you might not step in, and, on sufficient prospect of lucre, offer to take on the enterprise even if you have to shove your Shakespeare into the Savoy dustbin. It is a possible combination.

Frohman has now wiped himself out of the book of life by putting up "Rebecca Something or Other" at the Globe. I meant to have the Globe for the Androcles double event; and Frohman had better never have been born than thwart me in this design. I have abandoned all remorse in his regard. I cannot do business with babies. Come Erlanger and young Lee Shubert come! Shall I be faithless to Lillah or spare Frohman? Nay.

G.B.S.

The famous love episode between Bernard Shaw and Mrs. Patrick Campbell, which started on 27 June, the course of which is to be followed in the correspondence between them contained in Bernard Shaw and Mrs. Patrick Campbell (1952), marks the beginning of the end of the correspondence with Granville Barker. Not that Shaw ceased to write to his friend and collaborator, but their work together did not thereafter demand the constant attention that Shaw gave to all his dramatic affairs. This attachment to Mrs. Pat was personal as well as professional, and the extent of the personal disturbance to the dramatist is indicated in the letters to be read in the volume referred to, but there was also the interest of a dramatist, ceaselessly in search of instruments for the staging of his work. In the talented actress with whom he now became intimate, Shaw thought he had found one of the greatest interpreters of his creations. This is not the place to discuss this remarkable affair which has become a classic in the history of the theatre. What had happened so far as we are concerned is suggested by the remark in Shaw's first love letter to the actress, "Lillah is a widow in a manner of speaking," by which he meant that she, Mrs. Pat, had captured him from Barker for her own theatre. Only "in a manner of speaking," however, for the friendship continued, and the affection Shaw had for both the Barkers did not diminish; but there was a change, and the new direction of his mind and heart made all the difference to the future of those concerned.

The Lillah McCarthy-Granville Barker Shakespeare season at the Savoy Theatre opened on 21 September 1912 with The Winter's Tale. No letters from Shaw about this or the other Shakespeare productions survive. He attended the rehearsals regularly, however.

Shaw's little play Overruled was given in a triple bill by Charles Frohman at the Duke of York's Theatre on 14 October, a venture which as the following letter shows had failed. The dramatist was proposing that the piece should go with Galsworthy's Eldest Son into the bill at the Kingsway. Henry Kistemaeckers' play called Instinct was brought to the Duke of York's. Shaw was rehearsing Caesar and Cleopatra with Forbes-Robertson at Liverpool. He had written a new prologue.

I have found Boucicault a substitute for the failure of the Triple Bill, which is perishing on £800 a week—a very effective Kistemaeckers played here by Aubrey Smith and Lilian Braithwaite. Overruled will therefore presently be homeless, and might fill up the Galsworthy bill if Barrie's Little Mary is too expensive.

I shall be back next week. Caesar tonight. Cleop. is now very fascinating. With my new business Eysolt will receive a governess or companion.

G.B.S.

Barker was on holiday in Italy and Shaw was producing single-handed John Bull's Other Island, *which was revived at the Kingsway Theatre on 26 December.* The Secret Woman *was Eden Phillpott's censored play. Barker's production of* Twelfth Night *was being performed at the Savoy Theatre. Ethel Levey was appearing in the* Hullo, Ragtime! *at the Hippodrome Theatre where the J. M. Barrie skit referred to,* The Dramatists Get What They Want, *was given.*

Xmas Day 1912. 10 Adelphi Terrace,
W.C.

I can do no more with J. B., it must trouble through tomorrow as best it can. The scenery is frankly grotesque: such an orgie of red lengths and pink lines and impossible rostrums covered with obvious old yacht sails dyed scarlet, such penny theatre wings, were never seen in any theatre. As to the sky, it is beyond all description. It is the back of the panorama from the Secret Woman. McClure stimulated to insane excesses by me, first covered it with flaming vermilion clouds. When he realized that they wouldnt move as at Bayreuth and that the sky had to do for Acts III and IV he tried to paint the clouds out, and now they look like claret stains. The rise of the curtain on Act II will be the signal for a shriek of delirious laughter, which will culminate when the grasshopper is simulated by a watchman's rattle. (Ive tried everything in vain.) You'd simply die. As to the interiors, I have papered your old flats passably at eighteen-pence a piece. With luck the cast ought to pull through. I have got Calvert better than he ever was before, but he'll probably relapse hopelessly at the first sound of applause. The rest *should* be rather over than under the old mark. What they actually will be Heaven knows. Luckily we did not engage Austin for Haffigan: he has just dropped dead. Lillah is alright: her cold has gone; and she is the better for her expedition. She had a hideous crossing. Charlotte is at Edstaston. I am afraid I cant joint you in Venice. If only I'd bought a new Itala 40 h.p. a month ago I'd do it; but I cant trust the old machine. She cant tackle the mountains as she used to. And my arrears of work are terrible. J. B. has been a crusher. Also I cannot bear to go far from Illyria. Orsino was simply not in it with

G.B.S.

As to Barrie, there may be no hurry; but surely it would be a lift to her to have the Shrew produced first in London. At all events he had better ask her.

His censorship skit went very well in the Hippodrome Rome, which must have cost enough to mount six Winter's Tales. You were introduced in the first act of it in Greek costume.

They have a frightfully clever Jewess there named Levey. She and Heggie get the last inch out of Barrie's scene. She will be a [indecipherable word] some day. Hope you can read this.

I cant.

He then relates an episode when, driving his car in Hertford-shire, he was nearly killed. The Shaws were on the way to another Irish holiday.

The Old Cottage Loaf Hotel,
Dunstable. 26th March 1913.

Fate has suddenly turned malignant. At 12.20 we started from Ayot in splendid weather on splendid roads in high spirits, the car going brilliantly. At 13.20 I had to decide instantly whether I would smash another car to bits and kill two women and probably two more also, not to mention the effect of the collision on ourselves, or to take a desperate chance of saving the other car and wrecking myself only. I wrecked myself. I charged a clump of hummocks, a drain, and a telegraph pole, and came to a standstill buried in the hummocks, without a scratch or a broken bone, with my front axle ruined, my nearside spring in potato chips, my mudguard crumpled like paper, my tool box and footboard exploded, my electric horn in ribbons, and Charlotte's convalescent high spirits dashed to fragments. I spare you the details of the towing to Dunstable. I phoned to Harrods for a car to go on with. Hours passed: no car. I phoned again and was answered that the car—*your* car and *your* driver, as it turned out—was on the way. And when it arrived two hours late, having compelled us to stay for the night here, lo! the driver was on the verge of delirium tremens, and was thrown out of the hotel after smiting the waiter and making himself generally impossible. I have phoned Daimlers for a sober substitute and another car; but I have no faith now in the success of our expedition. On Saturday I shall be at the L. & N.W. Hotel, Holyhead, before crossing by the afternoon boat. My address in Ireland will be

% The Right Hon. Horace Plunkett, Kilteragh, Foxrock, Co. Dublin.

G.B.S.

While Twelfth Night *was still running arrangements were at last in hand for the production of* Androcles and the Lion, *which Shaw had written with a principal part for Lillah McCarthy. As the letters show, the Barkers were not intending to finish with Shakespeare. With Lord Howard de Walden's backing, who was more than pleased with the way things had gone at the Little and were going at the Kingsway, the St James's Theatre was taken from George Alexander for a period of four months. There the Shaw play was to be done and there Shaw and Barker intended to try out the repertory idea, with the intention that such a theatre should permanently be established in London.*

The "revolving business" was required for staging the second act of Androcles and the Lion. *The question of fees arose because another piece was to be done with it.*

Kilteragh, Foxrock. 3rd April 1913.

I dont want breaks: Why should I? But the more I think of

that revolving business the less I see how it can be done, unless, like Maeterlinck at St. Wandrilles, we shift the audience. The difficulty is that the people all keep their places. Unless they revolve with the box and staircase there will have to be a black-out.

It would be very much better to have Lillah and Ainley; but, of course, they are not indispensable for those two parts, though we will need important substitutes. I dont think we can afford to put the Androcles bill into repertory for the first bite in America unless it is a failure.

The solution of the fee difficulty is to double the fees, or at least raise them to Carton-Pinero-Barrie level. You cant expect masterpieces at 5, $3\frac{3}{4}$ and $2\frac{1}{4}$. How are I to live?

Yes: Quartermaine will be all right for the Hemperor.

G.B.S.

% The Rt. Hon. Sir Horace Plunkett,
Kilteragh, Foxrock, Co. Dublin,
31st March 1913.

I believe I owe you various sums for theatre tickets; but I can remember nothing except £2:2:—for a box for the Russian Ballet, and a stall which I guess at 15/-. The rest you must treat me to.

After the smash and the adventure of the drunken chauffeur I completed the triad by a blighting headache. We then got across here without mishap. This house, which looks exactly like a picture by Picasso, is delightfully situated. I wish you were here. Do you know Plunkett?

Charlotte is in high spirits—almost in health. The domestic fiend of the last few months has become a green-eyed angel of the fireside. She actually gibes at her rival.

Is the Barrett play a success?

Revises of Androcles have just come from the printer. Has that matter advanced at all? What about Lawd Ahrd? On going through the play again I have become convinced that you would make a perfect Androcles. You would pat the lion to perfection; and you could turn on your ghastly terror-of-death effect in the arena. So if you like to understudy Heggie, or even overstudy him, £5 an act shant part us.

Is Barrie going to be faithful to Stella in the matter of that murderess play, or will he betray her with Irene? I want to know before I move again in the matter of Pygmalion. I really dont see why Pygmalion should go out of the family. If we cant manage Mrs. Pattikins, whom (of the first order) can we manage? "Love will find out the Way."

Lillah, I assume, is in Trafalgar Bay.

G.B.S.

After the two Shakespeare productions at the Savoy there was the intention to tackle the tragedies, Macbeth *being one of the plays in mind, and a good deal of preparatory work was done on the play. The two theatres were the Kingsway and the St. James'. After all,* Pygmalion *was not done until Beerbohm Tree put it on at His Majesty's Theatre on 11 April 1914, with himself and Mrs. Patrick Campbell in the company.* The New Statesman, *founded by the Sidney Webbs and Bernard Shaw started publication on 12 May 1913 with Clifford Sharp as editor.*

Kilteragh, Foxrock, Co. Dublin.
10th Apl. 1913.

We start from here on Friday evening and cross to the L. & N.W. Hotel, Holyhead, where we shall spend the night. On Saturday morning we start for Ayot, which we shall not reach before Sunday evening. We come up to London on Monday.

The obvious reason for doubling the fees is that it costs me as much to live when I provide half the evening's entertainment as when I provide the whole. Nothing simpler. An alternative is to run two theatres and let me provide half at each. Then the argument will be on your side.

I am keen on Barrie because I am by no means sure of Androcles. It may prove simply an irritant. I have not read Barrie's interpolations, though I know their tenor from his description; but I count a good deal on Shakespear with his character study of Petruchio seriously handled by you in your XII Night style. There will be 3 authors; and the dead one may hold his own if the live ones fail.

I am by no means against opening with Macbeth if you think

189

you have a powerful performance of it in hand; but on the whole, its best place may be in reserve in case the Androcles bill goes wrong.

I have read both And. & Pyg. here aloud. They seem to me highly unsatisfactory. I believe I was slightly mad last year.

If the Androcles bill catches on, you will not change it after four weeks; you could not afford it either pecuniarily or nervously. If it doesnt, then you can make a repertorial virtue of necessity.

Albert Rotherstein will do as well as anybody else within reach. If his designs are wrong, I'll alter them.

I cant fix up Pygmalion for the Kingsway, not being the manager of that temple of art. Mrs. Pattikins is back at 33 Kensington Square; and you had better approach her on the subject. She does not doubt Barrie's fidelity; but she does (I gather) doubt whether she will be able to hold out if his play is not to be produced until after the next Peter Pan revival. The interim is yours.

Loraine cables for permission to do the first act of Superman in vaudeville. I have replied "An excellent idea."

Forbes announces Caesar for Monday, when I shall be speaking in Gravesend, and Thursday, when I shall be speaking in Ipswich.

Is Wish Wynne too expensive to understudy Galatea? If so, we shall have to insure Mrs. P. as all our eggs will be in one basket.

The New Statesman looks as if it would devour me. I have had to provide three articles for the first number. I'm not going to sign anything in it. Gerald Gould has done a good article on the censor for the second number—several excellent new jibes.

I wired today that I would sign the whip.

I note that your boat is on the shore and your bark is on the sea.

G.B.S.

Androcles and the Lion, a Fable Play, was performed at the St. James's Theatre on 1 September 1913 before a distinguished audience. It had been rehearsed by Barker, for Shaw was at the climax of his love affair with Mrs. Patrick Campbell, but at the dress rehearsal Shaw came along to find Barker's production too quiet, too slow, too detailed, and devoid of the flamboyant display and acting exuberance he most valued. Shaw worked for some hours, then went home to bed, leaving Barker to put together again what he had left in pieces.

There was a distinguished first-night audience including Ellen Terry, H. G. Wells, John Masefield, John Galsworthy and others. "Laughter long and loud and even thundered in the St. James's Theatre" said the St. James's Gazette next day, but while there was much praise no play by Shaw aroused more violent opposition—it could not be called criticism. "An enormously clever insult thrown in the face of the British people," declared the Daily Telegraph. "A burlesque of belief. . . . What is the stage come to?" cried the Daily Sketch. "Everything is turned to ridicule, to sardonic joking. Christianity is scoffed at, martyrdom is lampooned, the beauty of faith is the subject of jeers," lamented the God-fearing Daily Express. "There were some hisses," remarked the Evening News, while The Times was genially above all such nonsense: "of course it is the lion's evening. Was ever beast so fortunate? . . . we mean in being the one character in the whole range of Shavian drama who never talks." Finally the Church Times was ablaze with "angry grief" and "indignation" at "a bolder and more direct affront to Christianity than any play of the past." There was, of course, heavy newspaper correspondence in which Shaw joined. Shaw said he wrote the play partly for children, and although much of it is over their heads, that, declared Shaw, was the way in which to write for them. Certainly children like it, and it has become the most generally popular of the author's plays. Writing of it at the time, H. G. Wells said it was the only decent representation of Christianity he "had ever seen on the stage," and the only play for children at present in London. The Shaws went away for a Continental holiday immediately after the opening of the play.

Grand Hotel, Biarritz.
4th Oct. 1913.

My holiday has by this time utterly wrecked my health. A headache has all but finished me. Charlotte is struggling bravely against extreme weariness and indisposition. Otherwise I should have written yesterday or the day before. As it is I can hardly write now.

It seems to me that you are caught in the usual cleft stick. If you take off Androcles, you will confess a failure where there has really been a record success; and the chances of improving matters by a revival of The Witch or anything else are obviously quite desperate. If you keep it on, you will lose money unless the business goes up, which does not seem at all likely. Under these circumstances it seems to me that the best thing to do is to tell Howard how the matter stands, and ask him does he consider that the show is good enough to back until the end of the St. James's tenancy; that is, whether he will face the loss for the sake of the work. If he will, I am willing to forego all fees whilst he is losing.

I am glad that Wells has struck the right note as to the lion and the children; but I suppose Xmas is the only time to exploit that.

Is there any other theatre that would take on Androcles if you could let the St. James's or induce Alexander to take it off your hands? By the way, Alick ought to be informed of the state of the case frankly. He might be able to make some suggestion. The play is evidently a huge moral success; and it is rather a pity to discredit it by a commercial failure which is largely artificial.

I am not at this moment equal to an elaborate economic argument; but your notion that the author must give way to everyone else is not washable. There are various rent yielding monopolies in question: the ground landlord's monopoly, the monopoly of the prestige of the theatre, the author's monopoly, and your monopoly of Barkerized production. Now to allow the first two monopolists their rash rent (and more) without question, and then to tell the author that there is only half pay (if that) left for him, is not a position that the Society of Authors can countenance, without stultifying itself. However, the matter does not press now, as I am, as aforesaid, willing to drop all fees if Howard will see you through without a change of program and loses thereby.

G.B.S.

What Barker did was to experiment with repertory for some weeks, first at the St. James's, afterwards at the Savoy; then came the famous production of A Midsummer Night's Dream *on 6 February 1914, which ran until the middle of May. An attempt to find money to put the repertory on a permanent basis failed. The Kingsway Theatre, of which the Barkers had a long lease, continued, but then came the war, which put an end to everything. Shaw's letters became less frequent, for the two men were not working so closely together, and, except for a few late ones contained in the following pages, not one was preserved.*

6

Epilogue

When the first World War started Barker's spirits were at their lowest ebb. He saw no future for the theatre or for himself, and, after producing The Dynasts *at the Kingsway Theatre in November 1914, he accepted an invitation to be responsible for some productions in New York. No letters from Shaw at this period have survived. Barker and his wife went to New York in December 1914. In New York he fell in love with Helen Huntington but returned home with his wife in July 1915. Later that year he went back to the United States to lecture and then wrote to Lillah asking her to divorce him. There were many letters from Shaw during the period of great trouble for the Barkers, but Barker did not keep them. He spent much of his time with the Shaws. There is a letter from Shaw when Barker had returned to America for the second time.*

10, Adelphi Terrace,
London, W.C.
28th February 1917.

Your letter of the 29th January has just arrived. I have also had yours descriptive of Getting Married.

First, as to The Devil's Disciple. Faversham wanted to do it instead of Getting Married; but I said positively that I would not allow it to be played during the war, as the demand for it is clearly an attempt to exploit anti-English feeling. I forbade all authorizations of it by Miss Marbury's people; but I practically promised Faversham that he should have the refusal of it when the embargo was removed. Consequently I am afraid I can do nothing for John D. Williams in the matter.

Ann Elder "mistaking my instruction which within her brain did gyrate," or possibly through my giving her the wrong instructions, gave you Augustus instead of O'Flaherty. However, I have now got an official permit to export plays; so all that bother is over.

My elderly routine was violently upset at the end of January by an official invitation to visit the front. Under the circumstances I felt that I must regard this as an order, so after endless bother with passports and permits and tailors and bootmakers, behold me in trench boots and khaki in Ypres, in Arras, in St. Eloi, on the Somme front, riding in tanks, lunching with the C.I.C., teaing with Rawlinson, freezing for a night at Loraine's flying station (he is now back, and a Colonel, having got his wing), hobnobbing with Almroth, and performing stupendous conversational feats at all the mess tables from Bailleul to Amiens. I grieve to say that I enjoyed myself enormously in spite of temperatures that kept pretty close round 20 fah, and gave me my first taste of frostbite (fortunately a mild one). The artillery delighted me much more than Tchaikovsky's 1812; but it was a one-sided display; hardly anything came my way, even in Ypres. I am qualified for the Royal Irish Artillery as being distinctly one of "the boys that fear no noise." I crossed to Boulogne on the 28th January and returned on the 5th February. For the details and moral summing up, see The Daily Chronicle and whatever American paper Reynolds may sell the article to.

All this, and the subsequent writing ate up a solid four weeks.

As to Medley and money matters, words cannot describe the muddling of the bank. They insisted on doing the thing in two different and incompatible ways simultaneously; and in the end I very nearly missed converting my 4½% stock to the new 5¼ through their imbecility. However, I presume it's all right now. Poor Medley, between the Bank idiots on the one hand, and my explosions on the other, has had quite a time of it.

I am glad to see that L. is playing at last in a sketch. I saw Maggie a little while ago, and she told me, on the authority of Evelyn Weedon, who is or was down at Stansted, that L. was waking up in the nights in a manner which shewed that she was still taking things rather hardly. Is there any use in suggesting her to Faversham for the acrobat in Misalliance?

I am told in confidence, of which this is a breach, that there are serious official leanings towards an attempt to convince the neutrals of Europe that we can outdo Reinhardt when it comes to high art by sending out a specimen of our best, and that it is understood, for a wonder, that this conviction cannot be carried to the admirers of Reinhardt by Sir H. Tree. It seems to me that if you were called on for any duty of this kind you could not easily refuse: it would be your Pflicht to take the job on. I therefore give you the hint in extreme confidence, not knowing in the least whether the project will mature (there are no smart chatterbox ladies in it or anything of that sort), not so much lest it should take you by surprise as because you may be making plans and had better foresee all possibilities.

Ever

G.B.S.

P.S. Souls On Fifth is raging in The Fortnightly. Maggie is very hochnasig about it.
From G.Bernard Shaw to Granville Barker. (One must give these particulars now.)

The letter was intended to cheer up the unhappy Barker. Souls On Fifth *was a long short story that Barker had written in America and was published there. The long delayed matter of his divorce (because Lillah was refusing to take action) was at last put in hand, and the decree against him was secured by Lillah in April 1917. She had been refusing for more than a year, but at last could not withstand the advice to release him, in both their interests, by Shaw and all Barker's friends. He and Helen Huntington, who had divorced her husband, were married in London on 31 July 1918. During the latter part of this time Shaw had seen little of Barker and had written little to him, because Helen discouraged it. Having heard of the marriage Shaw wrote to Barker.*

Penlea, nr. Dartmouth, Devon.
26th Aug. 1918.

I am staying here with the Fabian Summer School until it breaks up on the 7th Sept, having put in ten days with Lady Scott sitting for a statuette at Streatley, and ten more with the Webbs at Prestaga, a place in Radnorshire with a very healthy air. Charlotte is at Parknasilla with her sister.

It would be convenient occasionally to know something about you. I surmise that you are married; but it is only a surmise. It is desirable that your friends should be in a position to make a positive affirmation on the subject. An effectation of ecstasy so continuous as to make you forget all such worldly considerations is ridiculous at your age. So just send me along any information that ought to be public, however briefly. I have refrained, with an exaggerated delicacy, from asking you questions for a year or so. Now I do ask them bluntly. People ask me questions; and there is not the same reason for not meeting them with a mystery that there was formerly for not giving them too much information.

When we were at Torcross I visited this place (which is about half way between it and Dartmouth) and had tea one afternoon. I forget whether you were with me. I play the bishop at the school, and swim and dance and lecture and so forth with Pickwickian geniality. Olivier is at Dartmouth, and comes over occasionally. Did you see his poem in The Nation.

I may possibly stay here for a while after the 7th; but I doubt it. Charlotte expects me to go on to Parknasilla; but I am not keen on it: it is a long and troublesome journey; and I had a thorough dose of it last year, not to mention that I am not in the best of humors with my countrymen. Ireland is now one huge Mutual Admiration Club of stupendous futility. When Plunkett has to admit that the Irish will not tolerate the Federal solution (mine, and the only possible one short of total and disastrous separation) because it would treat Ireland exactly as it would treat England and Scotland, and thereby implying that the first flower of the earth and first gem of the sea is no better than these comparatively negligible parishes, and has in fact no special problem, the matter goes beyond human patience.

197

Charlotte reports "a withering contempt for the British Government." Helpful, *that*.

ever
G.B.S.

The same year Shaw read his play, Back to Methuselah, *or a part of it to some friends, among whom Barker and Helen were included. He subsequently wrote to Barker as follows:*

Ayot St. Lawrence, Welwyn, Herts.
18th Dec. 1918.

Your state is more gracious than mine; for I, alas! am worse bored by the Brothers Barnabas than by their unfortunate family and rector. I shall have to get the picture better composed; but I don't think it will come to a Socratic dialogue pure and simple. The idea is not to get comic relief (they are not really comic, if you come to that); but to exhibit the Church, marriage, the family, and parliament under shorthand conditions before reproducing them under long lived conditions. The stuttering rector develops into an immoral archbishop and the housemaid into a Minister of Public Something or other. Clara I am not at all savage with; the notion is that a really capable and restlessly active minded woman, under the burden of housekeeping and the assaults of an idle beauty-cultivating woman on her husband, inevitably becomes a Clara, squabbling continually, but mysteriously keeping her grip on the man because in the final issue she is indispensable and there is nothing against her except that her daily worries have kept her intellect undeveloped whilst her interests lead her into subjects in which intellectual inadequacy is maddening. But until I succeed in making this plain, she and the rest seem dull and in fact are dull and irritating, just as in real life. To the end I may have to disregard the boredom of the spectator who has not mastered all the motifs, as Wagner had to do; but I daresay I shall manage to make the people more amusing, some of them more poetic, and all of them more intelligible than they now are in this first draft.

The girl who jars on her father (and on you) justified herself by jarring very surprisingly on Asquith. You see, if I make them all satisfactory, the reason for making them live 300 years vanishes. What I have to do is not to make them satisfactory; but to find an artistic treatment of their unsatisfactoriness, which will prevent its being as disagreeable to the audience as the real thing.

I was, I suppose, tired out when I read it; for it has never seemed quite so tedious before.

I did not pity you, as it is all in your day's work, but it was rather hard on Helen to have such a depressing beginning of my playreading.

G.B.S.

There was little more, for Barker's second wife could not stand Shaw and the friendship was virtually brought to an end. Barker wrote to him about the play when it was published, and wrote again after he had seen a performance of St. Joan. *Shaw doubtless replied, but his letters have not survived.*

There was also much trouble from Barker about Shaw's Foreword to Lillah McCarthy's book of reminiscences, Myself and My Friends, *but no letters are available. My account of all these events appears elsewhere.*

When Mrs. Shaw died, Shaw wrote a pathetic postcard to Barker, who was in New York, which concludes this correspondence.

4, Whitehall Court,
London,
S.W.1
14/9/43.

Charlotte died last Sunday, the 12th. September, at half past two in the morning. She had not forgotten you.

Since 1939 she has suffered much pain and lately some distress from hallucinations of crowds of people in her room; and the disease, a horror called osteitis deformans which bent and furrowed her into a Macbeth witch (an amiable one), was progressing steadily and incurably. But last Friday a miracle occurred. She suddenly threw off her years, her visions, her fur-

199

rows, her distresses, and had thirty hours of youth and happiness before the little breath *she* could draw failed. By morning she looked twenty years younger than you or I ever knew her.

It was a blessedly happy ending; but you could not have believed that I should be as deeply moved. You will not, I know, mind my writing this to you. She was 86. I am 87.   G.B.S.

To this postcard Barker replied but the letter has not survived. Barker died in Paris on 31 August 1946. He was sixty-eight. Shaw in his home at Ayot St. Lawrence heard the news announced in the B.B.C. Home Service News with sorrow. He died at Ayot St. Lawrence on 2 November 1950 at the age of ninety-four.

Index

Frohman, Charles, 55, 101, 183
Frohman Repertory Theatre, 148, 151, 152-167

Galsworthy, John, 111, 149, 174, 191
George V, King, 173, 174
George, A. E., 23, 28, 32, 34, 35, 36, 39, 53, 76, 104
Getting Married, 101, 106, 108, 118, 129, 156, 160, 194
Ghosts, 2
Gill, Basil, 75
Globe, The, 48
Goodhart, Porthos, 28, 32, 82
Good Hope, The, 12
Gore, Holmes, 69, 71, 75
Gorell, Lord, 156
Gould, Gerald, 190
Graves, Clotilde Inez Mary, 17, 19
Greenlaw, Nora, 52, 53, 125
Greet, (Sir) Ben, 5, 27, 76
Greet, Clare, 69, 71, 178
Gregory, Lady, 138, 167
Grein, J. T., 2, 122
Grossmith, George, 69
Grossmith, Weedon, 159
Gurney, Edmund, 65, 71, 73, 96, 103, 104, 105
Gwenn, Edmund, 52, 53, 71, 77, 102-3, 177

Hallard, C. M., 32, 66, 67, 149
Halston, Margaret, 15, 23
Hamilton, Mary, 81, 94, 102, 103
Hamlet, 179-180
Hankin, St. John, 52, 57, 77-8, 102, 103, 105, 111, 131, 140, 141-2
Harben, Hubert, 75, 149, 159
Harcourt, R. V., 152
Harcourt, Right Hon. Sir William, 41
Harding, J. Rudge, 76
Hare, (Sir) John, 76, 82, 128
Harrison, Frederick, 88, 101, 118-9
Harvey, (Sir) Martin, 20, 75, 160
Hawtrey, Charles, 75, 119
Haydon, Florence, 177
Headlam, Rev. Stewart, 33
Hearn, James, 69, 71, 76, 82, 115, 130-1
Heartbreak House, 155

Hedda Gabler, 75-7
Heggie, O. P., 149-50, 181
Heinemann, William, 56
Helen's Path, 164
Helmsley, C. T. H., 114
Hendrie, Ernest, 22, 24, 27, 34, 35
Hignett, H. R., 160
Hippolytus, 40, 46
Hobson, S. G., 140-1
Housman, Laurence, 118, 122, 124
How He Lied to her Husband, 23, 25, 40, 47, 68, 69
Huntington, Helen, 194, 196, 198

Ibsen, Henrik, 1, 2, 4, 7, 12, 17, 56
Independent Theatre, The, 2
Interior, 4
Irving, Ethel, 50
Irving, Sir Henry, 44, 179
Irving, H. B., 28, 75, 160
Irving, Laurence, 3, 75

James, Henry, 2
Joan of Arc, 84n.
John Bull's Other Island, 23-45, 47, 52, 54, 59, 61, 66, 70, 71, 84, 94, 95-6, 107-8, 130, 155, 174, 185-6
John Gabriel Borkman, 2
Jones, Henry Arthur, 1, 2, 31, 135
Joy, 104, 105
Justice, 163

Kearney, Kate, 24
Kelly, F. H., 76
Kendal, (Dame) Madge, 18
Kendal, Williams, 18
Kerr, Frederick, 57, 59, 76
Kinghorne, Mark, 24, 27
Kingston, Gertrude, 47, 171
Kingsway Theatre, 172, 180, 181, 182, 185, 187, 193, 194

Lablache, Luigi, 76, 103
Laceby, Arthur, 53
Lamborn, Amy, 61, 102
Last of the De Mullins, 131, 141, 142
Lauder, (Sir) Harry, 77
L'Aiglon, 8
League of Youth, The, 4
Lee, Auriol, 121, 124-5, 126, 130
Leno, Dan, 15
Levey, Ethel, 185, 186